# PRISONERS OF CONSCIENCE IN THE USSR:
## Their Treatment and Conditions

D1384760

AN
AMNESTY INTERNATIONAL
REPORT

**AMNESTY INTERNATIONAL** is a worldwide human rights movement which is independent of any government, political faction, ideology or religious creed. It works for the release of men and women imprisoned anywhere for their beliefs, colour, ethnic origin or religion, provided they have neither used nor advocated violence. These are termed "prisoners of conscience".

**AMNESTY INTERNATIONAL** opposes torture and capital punishment in all cases and without reservation. It advocates fair and speedy trials for all political prisoners.

**AMNESTY INTERNATIONAL** seeks observance throughout the world of the United Nations Universal Declaration of Human Rights and of the UN Standard Minimum Rules for the Treatment of Prisoners.

**AMNESTY INTERNATIONAL** has consultative status with the United Nations (ECOSOC), UNESCO and the Council of Europe, has cooperative relations with the Inter-American Commission on Human Rights of the Organization of American States and has observer status with the Organization of African Unity (Bureau for the Placement and Education of African Refugees).

**AMNESTY INTERNATIONAL** is financed by its members throughout the world, by individual subscription and by donations.

# PRISONERS OF CONSCIENCE IN THE USSR:
## Their Treatment and Conditions

Amnesty International Publications
53 Theobald's Road London WC1X 8SP England
1975

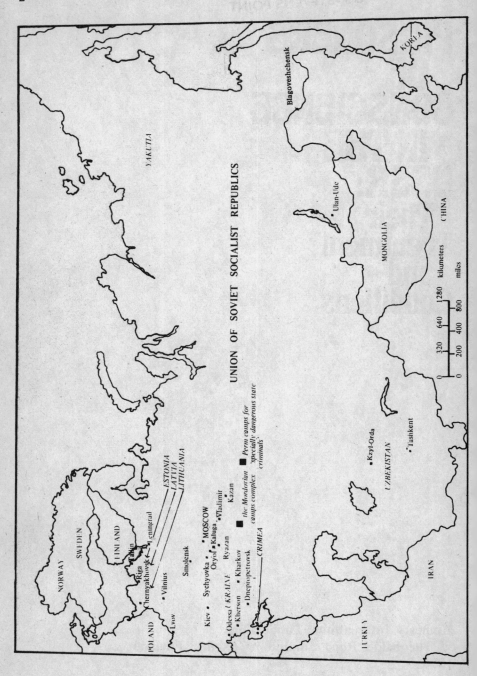

UNION OF SOVIET SOCIALIST REPUBLICS

KOREA

Blagoveshchensk

YAKUTIA

Ulan-Ude

CHINA

MONGOLIA

kilometers
miles

0    320    640    1280
0    200    400    800

Kzyl-Orda

Tashkent

UZBEKISTAN

IRAN

TURKEY

NORWAY

SWEDEN

FINLAND

Leningrad

ESTONIA
LATVIA
LITHUANIA

Tallinn
Riga
Chernyakhovsk
Vilnius

Smolensk

MOSCOW
Oryol    Kaluga    Vladimir
Sychyovka              Kazan
Kiev                   Ryazan

Oдessa UKRAINE    Kharkov
POLAND    Kherson    Dnepropetrovsk
Lvov                  CRIMEA

■ Perm camps for
  'specially dangerous state
  criminals'

■ the Mordovian
  camps complex

# Contents

4

*Above:* An exterior view of the Chernyakhovsk special psychiatric hospital in Kaliningrad region.

*Below:* Partial view of the special psychiatric hospital in Kazan, Tatar ASSR.

# Introduction

*by Martin Ennals, Secretary General, Amnesty International*

In July 1974 representatives of the Association of Soviet Lawyers handed a copy of the Fundamentals of Soviet Corrective Labour Legislation to a delegation in Moscow from the International Executive Committee of Amnesty International. The lawyers stressed that, while an area of discretion existed within each penal institution of the Union of Soviet Socialist Republics, the "Fundamentals" themselves provided even better safeguards and conditions for the prisoners than those required by the United Nations' Standard Minimum Rules for the Treatment of Prisoners, which define international norms relating to prison conditions.

In accepting the Soviet document, the Amnesty International delegation emphasized that the rules would be studied carefully and compared with international standards. The delegation also advised the lawyers that a report on Soviet prison conditions was being written by Amnesty International, and it confirmed a previous assurance that both they and the appropriate Soviet authorities would be able to comment on the report before it was published.

This meeting in Moscow was one of a series of talks with distinguished leaders of the Soviet legal profession which have taken place since 1973. Amnesty International representatives have on several occasions provided the Soviet lawyers with lists of prisoners of conscience in the USSR whose cases Amnesty International has adopted. Discussions have included reference to prison conditions and to the UN Standard Minimum Rules for the Treatment of Prisoners — rules which are regularly supported and endorsed by the Soviet delegates to UN international conferences.

Representatives of the Association of Soviet Lawyers were shown an advance copy of this report at an international conference of lawyers in Algiers in April 1975. The draft typescript was then mailed to the chairman of the association, Lev Smirnov, in Moscow on 15 April. Mr Smirnov is also chairman of the Soviet Supreme Court. In a covering letter, Amnesty International indicated that it would welcome comments on the accuracy or interpretation of the facts in the report. Mr Smirnov's reply, dated 27th August 1975, is reproduced at the end of this report.

Although the report deals with prison conditions, Amnesty International's primary concern is for the unconditional release of all prisoners of conscience. It therefore welcomed the Soviet government's decision in September 1973 to ratify the UN International Covenant on Civil and Political Rights which includes provisions to safeguard the fundamental human rights of individual citizens. These safeguards are essentially similar to the guarantees contained in the Soviet Constitution. Regrettably, the Soviet criminal code contains apparently contradictory provisions (see pages 7-8) which permit the authorities to imprison political and religious dissenters.

One manifestation of this anomaly between accepted international law and the Soviet Constitution on the one hand and domestic criminal law on the other is that most of those who are now in prison in apparent violation of internationally accepted standards of human rights are, in fact, detained under the criminal code for offences against Soviet law. One of the purposes of the present report is to draw attention to these contradictions in the hope that Soviet lawyers and penologists will review their legal and penal practices and that the law will be amended to bring them into conformity with the recently ratified international covenants and with the Soviet Constitution itself.

The offer which Amnesty International made to the Soviet lawyers to take into account any errors of fact which may accidentally appear in the report is still valid. Indeed, changes in penal procedures and the amendment of certain of the laws relating to the treatment of persons in restriction who are said to be mentally ill and in need of treatment would radically affect the report itself — a situation which would be welcomed by all Amnesty International members and supporters, not least the writers of the report.

However, it is the conviction of Amnesty International that present conditions are as described in this report, and that in prisons, corrective labour colonies and psychiatric hospitals in the USSR, conditions fall below the international and national standards to which the Soviet Union subscribes.

Article 55 of the Fundamentals of Public Health Legislation of the USSR and the union republics in the field of public health, for example, lays down that "where an international treaty or agreement to which the USSR is a party established rules other than those contained in the public health legislation of the USSR and the union republics, the rules of the international treaty or agreement shall be applied". It is Amnesty International's hope that in regard to human rights and the treatment of prisoners the same principle will be applied.

# ARTICLES OF SOVIET CRIMINAL LAW WHICH RESTRICT THE EXERCISE OF FUNDAMENTAL HUMAN RIGHTS

Most Soviet prisoners of conscience are imprisoned for violations of six articles of Soviet criminal law:[1]

**Article 64:** This defines as an act of treason "flight abroad or refusal to return from abroad to the USSR".

**Article 70: Anti-Soviet Agitation and Propaganda.** Agitation or propaganda carried on for the purpose of subverting or weakening the Soviet regime or of committing particular, especially dangerous crimes against the state, or the circulation, for the same purpose, of slanderous fabrications which defame the Soviet state and social system, or the circulation or preparation or keeping, for the same purpose, of literature of such content, shall be punished by deprivation of freedom for a term of 6 months to 7 years, with or without additional exile for a term of 2 to 5 years, or by exile for a term of 2 to 5 years.

The same actions committed by a person previously convicted of especially dangerous crimes against the state or committed in wartime shall be punished by deprivation of freedom for a term of 3 to 10 years, with or without additional exile for a term of 2 to 5 years.

**Article 72: Organizational Activity Directed to Commission of Especially Dangerous Crimes against the State and also Participation in Anti-Soviet Organizations.** Organizational activity directed to the preparation or commission of especially dangerous crimes against the state, or to the creation of an organization which has as its purpose the commission of such crimes, or participation in an anti-Soviet organization, shall be punished in accordance with Articles 64-71 of the present code.

**Article 142: Violation of Laws on Separation of Church and State and of Church and School.** The violation of laws on the separation of church and state and of school and church shall be punished by correctional tasks for a term not exceeding one year or by a fine not exceeding 50 roubles.

The same acts committed by a person previously convicted of violation of laws on the separation of church and state and of school and church, as well as organizational activity directed to the commission of such acts, shall be punished by deprivation of freedom for a term not exceeding 3 years.

---

1. Reference here is to the Criminal Code of the Russian Soviet Federated Socialist Republic (RSFSR). The translation is from Harold J. Berman and James W. Spindler, *Soviet Criminal Law & Procedure: The RSFSR Codes* (Harvard University Press, Cambridge, Massachusetts, 1972). The same articles are to be found with different numeration in the criminal codes of each of the union republics of the USSR.

8

**Article 190-1: Circulation of Fabrications known to be False which Defame Soviet State and Social System.** The systematic circulation in an oral form of fabrications known to be false which defame the Soviet state and social system and, likewise, the preparation or circulation in written, printed or any other form of works of such content shall be punished by deprivation of freedom for a term not exceeding 3 years, or by correctional tasks for a term not exceeding one year, or by a fine not exceeding 100 roubles.

**Article 227: Infringement of Person and Rights of Citizens under Appearance of Performing Religious Ceremonies.** The organizing or directing of a group, the activity of which, carried on under the appearance of preaching religious beliefs and performing religious ceremonies, is connected with the causing of harm to citizens' health or with any other infringements of the person or rights of citizens, or with the inducing of citizens to refuse social activity or performance of civic duties, or with the drawing of minors into such groups, shall be punished by deprivation of freedom for a term not exceeding 5 years or by exile for a similar term with or without confiscation of property.

The active participation in the activity of a group specified in paragraph one of the present article, or the systematic propaganda directed at the commission of acts specified therein, shall be punished by deprivation of freedom for a term not exceeding 3 years, or by exile for the same term, or by correctional tasks for a term not exceeding one year.

*Note:* If the acts of persons stated in paragraph 2 of the present article, and the persons themselves, do not represent a great social danger, measures of social pressure may be applied to them.

# Profile of Five Prisoners of Conscience

The following brief case-histories are intended primarily to illustrate some typical reasons for which persons are arrested as a consequence of their political or religious views in the Soviet Union.

## *Paruir Airikian*

Paruir Airikian, born in 1949, is a native of Armenia, a Soviet Union republic south of the Caucasus mountains and bordering on Turkey and Iran. In recent years nationalist and civil rights groups have emerged among Armenians as among a number of other nationalities in the USSR.

In the summer of 1969 Mr Airikian, then a student at the Yerevan Polytechnical Institute, was among five young Armenians arrested and charged with forming an organization with "anti-Soviet aims" and with distributing "anti-Soviet" literature. At the group's trial in February 1970, the prosecution charged that the five had disseminated materials criticizing Soviet policy on nationalities and demanding creation of an independent Armenian state. All of the accused were found guilty and sentenced to imprisonment. As the alleged leader of the group, Mr Airikian received the heaviest sentence: 4 years' imprisonment in a strict regime corrective labour colony. While serving his sentence in a Mordovian colony, Mr Airikian was among nine prisoners who signed a collective appeal to the International Red Cross about their conditions of imprisonment.

Mr Airikian was released in the summer of 1973. In December of the same year, he was arrested again in connection with his effort to attend the trial of two friends. He was charged with violating the regulations restricting the movements of released prisoners. Early in 1974, a Yerevan court sentenced him to 2 years' imprisonment. (According to one report this sentence was one year.)

Mr Airikian was not sent at once to serve the sentence but was kept under investigation in a KGB prison. He was eventually charged with "anti-Soviet agitation and propaganda" and participation in an "anti-Soviet organization" and brought for trial before the Armenian Supreme Court on 22 October 1974.

According to an anonymous *samizdat* report on the trial, the prosecution brought in evidence a letter which Mr Airikian had written while serving his previous sentence and which had only been read by the Ministry of Internal

Affairs (MVD) censor who had confiscated it. The prosecution also referred to Mr Airikian's "contact with foreigners". In his final statement to the court, Mr Airikian denied having undertaken any organizational activity during his brief period of freedom. He stated: "The KGB workers told me that one way or another they would take care of me, that they would find a way to put me away since, they said, my mere presence among my comrades had an inspiring effect on them." Mr Airikian protested that he was being tried not for his actions but for his convictions.

Mr Airikian was sentenced to 7 years in a strict regime corrective labour colony, to be followed by 3 years' exile.

## Alexander Dmitrievich Feldman

Alexander Feldman, born in 1947, is a Ukrainian Jew. Until 1973 he was employed as a stoker in Kiev. In early 1972 he formally applied to be allowed to emigrate to Israel. Almost immediately, on 14 January 1972, police officials searched his flat and confiscated a quantity of literature. Emigration authorities refused his application to leave the country on the grounds that he knew "military secrets", although his military service had ended more than four years earlier. On three separate occasions in 1972 he was imprisoned for 15 days in connection with his efforts to protest publicly or to governmental bodies about the official refusal to allow him to emigrate.

On 18 October 1973, Mr Feldman was arrested and charged with "malicious hooliganism". It was alleged that he had attacked and caused physical injury to a woman and that he had violently resisted two male citizens who had come to the woman's assistance. He was tried in a local court on 23 November 1973 and sentenced to 3½ years' imprisonment in an intensified regime corrective labour colony.

A large amount of information is available concerning the official charges and the evidence used by the prosecution in the case against Mr Feldman. Taken by itself, this documentation supports Mr Feldman's contention that the case against him was a "frame-up". This interpretation is strengthened by the fact that Mr Feldman had previously been subject to frequent arrest and harassment and constant surveillance by police authorities in Kiev.

Amnesty International's view that the case against Mr Feldman was fabricated gains further support from events during and after his trial. At the last moment, the venue of the trial was shifted from a regular court building to the canteen of a factory, so that even his defence counsel had difficulty locating it. Mr Feldman's friends and relatives were not allowed to attend. His defence counsel, I.S. Yezhov, noted in his appeal on the case that the court hearing was "one-sided, superficial and lacking in objectivity". Only prosecution witnesses were questioned, and the court rejected the defence counsel's request that defence witnesses be called. The defence counsel was also obstructed in his efforts to question prosecution witnesses. Mr Yezhov's appeal was rejected, and he himself was almost immediately retired on a pension.

Mr Feldman is serving his sentence in a corrective labour colony in the Ukraine. There have been numerous reports that he is physically ill but has not received proper medical attention and has not been excused from hard physical labour. He has also been subjected to several periods in punishment cells and has been denied visits by members of his family.

### Kronid Arkadevich Lyubarsky

Kronid Arkadevich Lyubarsky, born in 1934, is an astro-physicist. He has written numerous scientific articles on such subjects as meteors, planets and space biology, many of which have been published in Soviet journals. He has also written three scientific books and translated several works into Russian, including *Galaxies* by Fred Hoyle. Until 1972 he worked at the Chornogolovka Institute of Solid State Physics near Moscow.

In January 1972, he joined a number of people arrested under "Case 24", the KGB's investigation of the publication and distribution of the *samizdat* human rights journal *A Chronicle of Current Events.* (As a result of this investigation and the arrests, searches and interrogations which proceeded under it, *A Chronicle of Current Events* stopped publication between October 1972 and May 1974.)

After eight months of preliminary detention, Mr Lyubarsky was brought to trial on 26 October 1972. He was charged with "anti-Soviet agitation and propaganda", the offence consisting in his having possessed and distributed several *samizdat* writings, including *A Chronicle of Current Events.* At the trial Mr Lyubarsky admitted having possessed and distributed a number of *samizdat* works, but denied that either his intent or the content of these materials was "anti-Soviet". In his final statement Mr Lyubarsky referred to the prosecution's having described as "slanderous" his (Mr Lyubarsky's) statement that Soviet citizens are put on trial for their convictions. Mr Lyubarsky described it as hypocrisy to claim that citizens had freedom of conviction but, at the same time, to prosecute them for uttering opinions which are distasteful to the authorities. He also stressed that socialism would be strengthened rather than weakened by the extension of freedom to criticize official policy.

Mr Lyubarsky's defence counsel argued that since no "anti-Soviet" intention on the defendant's part could be proved, the charge should be changed from "anti-Soviet agitation and propaganda" to "dissemination of fabrications known to be false which defame the Soviet state and social system". (The latter charge carries a less severe maximum sentence.) He also asked that the court's sentence be such as to allow Mr Lyubarsky to continue his scientific work. Both of these requests were rejected. Mr Lyubarsky was convicted under the original charge and sentenced to 5 years' imprisonment in a strict regime corrective labour colony.

Mr Lyubarsky was sent to serve the sentence in a Mordovian colony. Despite the fact that the greater part of his stomach was removed in surgery prior to his arrest, he has not been granted any special diet privileges. After a number of protests and hunger strikes, he was sent in October 1974 to serve the remainder of his sentence in Vladimir prison.

### Yakov Nikolayevich Pavlov

Yakov Nikolayevich Pavlov, born in 1935, worked until 1973 as a technical planner for a local government body in Taldy-Kurgan, in Kazakhstan. He is the father of eight children and a member of the dissenting wing of the

Evangelical and Christian Baptists. The dissenting Baptists refuse to accept some of the restrictions officially placed on religious activity in the early 1960s, particularly the restriction on their right to instruct their children in religion. In the autumn of 1973 Mr Pavlov was among a group of six dissenting Baptists arrested in Taldy-Kurgan and charged with a variety of criminal offences in connection with their religious activity, including violation of the laws on separation of church and state and school and church, and dissemination of lies defaming the Soviet state and social system.

At the trial of the six in February 1974, the prosecution charged that the accused had systematically spread religious propaganda, using for this purpose sermons, tape-recordings, and performances of religious verses and songs, some of which were "accompanied by musical instruments". The prosecution further charged that Mr Pavlov and two of his co-defendants had admitted having jointly "organized religious lessons for their under-age children", which according to the prosecution was in violation of the laws on "separation of church from state and of church from school". Basic evidence in the case included printed and tape-recorded sermons and songs confiscated from the defendants' homes and eye-witness testimony that the defendants' children regularly gathered together on Saturdays and Sundays and that one of the defendants (a woman named Ella Kasper, aged 24) sang religious songs at such gatherings.

The text of Mr Pavlov's final statement in court is available outside the USSR. In it he denied that he or his co-defendants had published literature defaming the Soviet state, but admitted that they had made and distributed copies of the Bible because these were in short supply. He admitted that he had criticized official policies and actions toward religious believers in the USSR, but he denied that any of his critical statements were untrue. He admitted having taught his children religious principles, but said that a faithful Christian was obliged to do so, just as a dedicated Marxist-Leninist was obliged by conscience to instruct his children in the principles of communism. He reminded the court that Lenin had defended the right of each person to profess and to preach his faith.

Mr Pavlov was convicted of criminal wrongdoings in his religious activity and sentenced to 5 years in a corrective labour colony. In addition, the court stripped him of his parental rights over four of his children. All of his co-defendants were also found guilty and sentenced to terms of imprisonment (although the sentence on one defendant was suspended), and three of them were similarly deprived of parental rights over some of their children.

Amnesty International does not know to which corrective labour colony Mr Pavlov was sent to serve his sentence.

## Irina Stasiv-Kalynets

Irina Stasiv-Kalynets, born in 1940, is a Ukrainian poetess. After graduating from Lvov University, she worked first as a teacher and then as a lecturer in Ukrainian language and literature in the preparatory faculty of Lvov Polytechnical Institute. Her verses for children were published in a number of official periodicals, as were the poems of her husband Igor Kalynets, who in the 1960s received high praise from critics in Czechoslovakia and Poland. They are parents of a teen-aged daughter, Dzvinka.

*Left:* Kronid
Lyubarsky

*Right:* Irina Stasiv-
Kalynets

Both Mrs Stasiv-Kalynets and her husband became victims of official repression of Ukrainian nationalist and human rights advocates which culminated in a wide-scale campaign of arrests and job dismissals in 1972 and 1973. On a number of occasions in 1970 and 1971, they protested to Soviet authorities about the imprisonment of the Ukrainian historian Valentyn Moroz and the micro-biologist Nina Strokata-Karavanskaya, both of whom were convicted of "anti-Soviet agitation and propaganda". Mrs Stasiv-Kalynets had also taken part in the formation of a small Citizens' Committee in Defence of Nina Strokata, and around this time she was dismissed from her job.

In January 1972, Irina Stasiv-Kalynets was herself arrested and charged with "anti-Soviet agitation and propaganda". Amnesty International does not know the precise substance of the accusations against her, but Mrs Stasiv-Kalynets has always denied their validity. She was tried in July 1972 in what was effectively a closed court session in Lvov. She was found guilty and sentenced to 6 years' imprisonment in an ordinary regime corrective labour colony, to be followed by 3 years in exile. The following month her husband was arrested. He, too, was subsequently convicted of "anti-Soviet agitation and propaganda" and sentenced to 6 years' imprisonment and 3 years' exile. Their daughter has been left in the care of relatives.

Mrs Stasiv-Kalynets is serving her sentence in a colony for women in the Ukraine. She has been involved in a number of appeals to authorities for extension of prisoners' rights. For example, in September 1974 she and several fellow-inmates asked permission to transfer some of their labour-earnings to a Soviet fund for victims of the Chilean junta. This request was refused, as had been their earlier request for the right to take part in religious services to mark Easter.

Mrs Stasiv-Kalynets was reported in 1974 and 1975 to be suffering from a serious condition affecting her liver and kidneys. Efforts by her family to send her medicines and warm clothing have been blocked by postal authorities or by the colony's administration.

## A NOTE ON SOURCES

In this investigation of Soviet prison conditions, Amnesty International has relied primarily on two types of sources: officially published materials and accounts by prisoners themselves, their families and friends.

Officially published sources include legal texts, official commentaries on legal texts, and works by Soviet jurists and scholars whose writings bear the official approval necessary for publication. Such sources have provided Amnesty International with much essential information, particularly regarding the official principles and mechanisms prescribed to govern the operation of Soviet penal institutions.

However, the official texts have several limitations. In the USSR, as in other countries, such texts provide almost no information about the particular treatment of prisoners of conscience. Furthermore, they provide very little in the way of a concrete description of life in Soviet penal institutions. It is just such information which must be sought in statements by prisoners and ex-prisoners themselves and by their acquintances and families. This type of material is mostly available in the form of *samizdat,* writings published and distributed without official sanction and by private individuals.

The objection may be raised that the authors of *samizdat* accounts of prison life are biased because of their opposition to some aspects of the Soviet system. While this consideration must always be taken into account, the available *samizdat* documents are generally highly credible records. These documents have been written at different times by many people in places remote from one another. There is a high degree of mutual corroboration among the documents and also between them and personal accounts given by ex-prisoners who have left the USSR. To ascribe this corroboration of fact to coincidence would be naive. To ascribe it to deliberate fabrication would be to assume a conspiracy of enormous proportions.

The available *samizdat* material taken as a whole provides us with convincing documentation of life in Soviet prison institutions such as is not provided in the official sources.

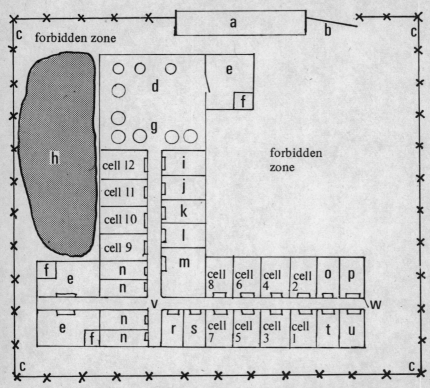

**Ground plan of zone number 1 (special regime) in camp complex ZhKh 385 in Mordovia**

*Key*

a  Guard-house
b  Gates
c  Fence
d  Work area, 14m x 12m x 3.2m
e  Excersize yards
f  Latrines
g  Grinding machines
h  Permanent pool of stagnant water and industrial waste
i  Censor
j  Camp head
k  KGB office
l  Head of prisoner supervision
m  Medical department
n  Punishment cells
o  Store, stall, barber, library

p  Warders' room
r  Baths
s  Hand basins
t  Hospital punishment cell
u  Washing-up room
v  Corridors
w  Entrance

This general plan of special regime colony ZhKh 385-1 was originally sketched by prisoner Boris Penson in 1974. (*Not to scale.*)

# Soviet Criminal Law and Prisoners of Conscience

Neither current Soviet law nor official Soviet policy statements recognize the concept of "prisoners of conscience" or that of "political prisoners". Public references even to the possible existence of political prisoners in the USSR are extremely rare. In 1959, Nikita S. Krushchev, then First Secretary of the Central Committee of the Communist Party of the Soviet Union and Chairman of the USSR Council of Ministers, remarked: "There are no political prisoners in Soviet prisons today."[1]

Soviet authorities have not always denied that Soviet citizens are liable to arrest purely on political grounds. The criminal codes legislated in the first decade of Soviet power specifically provided for arrest, conviction and imprisonment on political grounds. The practice of political imprisonment on a massive scale was one of the principle characteristics of Soviet public life at least until 1953. This fact was not concealed at the time, and it has been acknowledged by Soviet leaders on many occasions since the death of Stalin. Events have shown that, official denials notwithstanding, the practice of imprisoning people for political and religious activity remains entrenched in the USSR.

The main legal documents relevant to this question are:
- The Constitution of the USSR (1936).
- The Fundamentals of Criminal Law of the USSR and the Union Republics, legislated in 1958.[2]

---

1. *Pravda*, 28 January 1959.
2. The Fundamentals of Soviet Union legislation set down the basic legislation norms for a given branch of the law, such as criminal law, criminal procedural law, marriage and family law, penitentiary law, etc. The Fundamentals for many branches of Soviet law have been published together in English in *Fundamentals of Legislation of the USSR and Union Republics* (Progress Publishers, Moscow, 1974).

— The criminal codes legislated in each union republic between
1959 and 1961 on the basis of the Fundamentals of Criminal
Law of the USSR and the Union Republics.[3]

— The Fundamentals of Criminal Procedure of the USSR, legislated
in 1958.

— The Codes of Criminal Procedure legislated in each union republic
after 1958 on the basis of the Fundamentals of Criminal Procedure
of the USSR and the Union Republics.

(The legislation governing actual prison conditions will be discussed below).

## Political Offences

The 1960 criminal code replaced criminal legislation which had been in existence since 1926. The 1926 code was devised in part as a class weapon in the
fledgling Soviet state's years of struggle. It distinguished between ordinary and
"counter-revolutionary" (political) crimes, and called for much stronger
penalties for the latter.

Article 58 of the 1926 code provided blanket charges against anyone even
remotely suspected of representing a threat to the survival of Bolshevik rule.
Furthermore, some provisions in the 1926 code made legal the arrest and sen-
tencing of persons who were known to have committed no crime.[4] This phenomenon sprang from the primacy assigned to the interests of the state and to the
survival of Bolshevik power. In this situation, the law was an instrument of
political power. Interpretation and application of its provisions were always
subject to the political demands of the moment. The leading jurist A.A.
Piontkowsky, writing in 1947, made it clear that for political reasons, people
could be sentenced under criminal law in the absence even of suspicion that
they had committed a crime.

Of course, sometimes for these or those considerations of a political
nature it is necessary to apply compulsory measures to persons who have
not committed any crime but who on some basis or another (their past
activity, their ties to a criminal environment, etc) are socially dangerous.[5]

The 1926 criminal code was amended many times between 1929 and 1936,
and in such a way as to make it even more repressive. The infamous Article
58 was used to cover the arrest of countless persons, often on no logical basis
other than the convenience of the police organs. From 1934 until Josef Stalin's

3. Union republic codes are legislated in each republic for each branch of law for
which USSR Fundamentals are legislated. Most union republic codes are not made
available by Soviet publishing agencies in translated form. The RSFSR Criminal
and Criminal Procedural Codes are available in English-language translation in
Harold J. Berman and James W. Spindler, *Soviet Criminal Law and Procedure*
(Harvard University Press, Cambridge, Massachusetts, 1972). Since the union
republic criminal codes are generally identical to one another, we shall cite the
RSFSR criminal code as representative of all union republic criminal codes. The
RSFSR (Russian Soviet Federated Socialist Republic) is the largest union republic
in the USSR. In quoting articles of the RSFSR Criminal Code and the RSFSR
Code of Criminal Procedure, the translation used will be that in Berman and
Spindler, ibid.

4. RSFSR Criminal Code (1926), Article 7.

5. A.A. Piontkowsky, *Stalinskaya Konstitutsia i Proyekt Ugolovnogo Kodeksa
SSSR* (Moscow, 1947), pages 15-16.

death in 1953 a three-man special board of the NKVD (People's Commissariat of Internal Affairs[6]) was empowered to arrest, investigate, try, sentence and execute sentence on persons suspected of political opposition. The special board worked in secret in the absence of the accused and without need to consult any court or the legal codes.

After Stalin's death in 1953, there was a deep reaction against the arbitrary terror from which no one had been secure. Various piecemeal reforms were undertaken until the new criminal legislation was formulated at the end of the 1950s. The 1960 criminal code represented a major transformation of the Soviet legal system, a fact of which Soviet jurists are very proud.

The 1960 criminal code is not a "revolutionary" document — that is, it is not overtly intended as a weapon for one faction, party or class but as a law to be applied evenly to everyone in Soviet society. One consequence of this is that the 1960 code does not recognize any distinction between criminal and political offences. To do so would be to hint at the continuing existence of political opposition in the USSR, whereas according to official doctrine there is no social basis for such opposition. (This doctrine explains why the Soviet media have felt free to condemn Chile for not distinguishing between criminal and political prisoners, while not recognizing this distinction as valid in the USSR.)

Unlike its predecessors, the 1960 code stipulates that a person can be sentenced only if he has been tried in a court of law and proven guilty of an act specifically designated by law as a crime at the time of its commission.[7]

The 1960 Code of Criminal Procedure also contains strong guarantees of the rights of the accused. For example, the revulsion against earlier practice is very clearly expressed in the prohibition of night-time interrogation.[8] Furthermore, the same code limits the types of crimes which the KGB (Committee of State Security) and MVD are empowered to investigate and stipulates that the investigations must be under the supervision of the State Procuracy.[9] The crimes which the KGB can investigate are mostly in the criminal code's section "Especially Dangerous Crimes Against the State" (Articles 64-73). This is the section under whose articles many political prisoners are convicted.

The strong role of the procuracy in assuring observance of legality is affirmed by the 1960 criminal code and the 1961 Code of Criminal Procedure. The procuracy is a highly centralized organ, with the USSR Procurator-General (presently Roman Rudenko) appointed by and responsible only to the USSR Supreme Soviet, and with the Procurator-General appointing all procurators of the republics. In turn, the latter appoint to local, regional, city, district) procurators. The reason for this strong centralization is to free the procuracy from the control of local organs and thus enable it to exercise an autonomous supervisory function. This independence of the procurators is required specifically in Article 117 of the USSR Constitution.

6.   In 1946 the People's Commissariats were renamed "Ministries". The NKVD thus became the MVD: Ministry of Internal Affairs.
7.   RSFSR Criminal Code, Article 3.
8.   RSFSR Code of Criminal Procedure, Articles 123, 150.
9.   Ibid., Articles 125, 126.

The law (especially the 1955 Statute on Procuracy Supervision) gives the procuracy considerable power of supervision over the execution of justice. The procuracy can protest against any official order, instruction or decree which it considers to be in breach of the law. It can protest against the conduct of investigations and prosecution in criminal cases. In fact, the procuracy itself conducts the investigation of most kinds of criminal cases. In all criminal investigations, the officers of the procuracy, according to the law, must satisfy themselves that the law is being rigorously observed and "strictly watch out that not a single citizen is subjected to illegal or unfounded criminal prosecution or to any other unlawful restriction of rights".[10] Finally, the procuracy has very broad supervisory rights over court procedures and decisions and over the operation of penal institutions.

Nonetheless, both the written Soviet law and its application are still subject to considerations of political "expediency" which often dictate that abstract legal and constitutional principles must be sacrificed to political goals.

The Soviet Constitution of 1936 guarantees all Soviet citizens a number of human rights, including "freedom of religious worship" (Article 124), "freedom of speech", "freedom of the press", "freedom of assembly, including the holding of mass meetings", and "freedom of street processions and demonstrations" (Article 125). Similarly, Article 17 guarantees every union republic the right to secede from the Soviet Union, implying that citizens of any republic have the right to advocate such secession.

These rights are not officially recognized as absolute. Leonid Brezhnev, General Secretary of the Communist Party of the Soviet Union, said in October 1973:

> Soviet laws afford our citizens broad political freedoms. At the same time they protect our system and the interests of the Soviet people from any attempts to abuse these freedoms.[11]

Obviously vital is the official policy as to what constitutes "abuse" of human rights. In Soviet practice today, the use of speech, press or assembly to express or act upon beliefs or moral values incompatible with official policy and doctrine is liable to be treated as such "abuse". Likewise, any use of these rights to propagate the secession of a union republic or to advocate such an increase in a republic's autonomy as would reduce the established degree of central control is subject to severe sanctions.

Despite the absence of legal distinction between "political crimes" and "common law crimes", the present Soviet criminal codes list a number of crimes which are clearly political in character and which directly infringe upon the political rights of Soviet citizens. For example, Article 70 of the RSFSR Criminal Code reads:

> **Anti-Soviet Agitation and Propaganda.** Agitation or propaganda carried on for the purpose of subverting or weakening the Soviet regime [*vlast'*] or of committing particular, especially dangerous

10. Statute on Procuracy Supervision (24 May 1955), *Vedomosti Verkhovnogo Soveta SSSR*, Number 9, 1955, Article 17.
11. Text in L.I. Brezhnev, *For a Just, Democratic Peace, For the Security of Nations and International Cooperation* (Novosti Press, Moscow, 1973) page 39.

crimes against the state, or the circulation, for the same purpose
of slanderous fabrications which defame the Soviet state and social
system, or the circulation or preparation or keeping, for the same
purpose, of literature of such content, shall be punished by deprivation of freedom for a term of 6 months to 7 years, with or without
additional exile for a term of 2 to 5 years, or by exile for a term of 2 to
5 years.

The same actions committed by a person previously convicted of
especially dangerous crimes against the state or committed in wartime
shall be punished by deprivation of freedom for a term of 3 to 10
years, with or without additional exile for a term of 2 to 5 years.[12]

**Article 72 reads: Organizational Activity Directed to Commission of Especially
Dangerous Crimes Against the State and Also Participation in Anti-
Soviet Organizations.** Organizational activity directed to the preparation
or commission of especially dangerous crimes against the state, or to the
creation of an organization which has as its purpose the commission
of such crimes, or participation in an anti-Soviet organization, shall
be punished in accordance with Article 64-71 of the present code.[13]

Soviet authorities apparently found these articles to be inadequate in the face
of the legal issues raised at the famous 1966 trial of Andrei Sinyavsky and Yuly
Daniel, two writers accused of writing and circulating books containing "anti-
Soviet propaganda". Both the accused defended themselves against this charge
by arguing that their writings were in no way motivated by "anti-Soviet intent".
Despite the opinion of Soviet commentators[14] that "anti-Soviet intent" must
be shown for a person to be found guilty under Article 70, and despite the
prosecution's manifest difficulty in showing "anti-Soviet intent", Mr Sinyavsky
and Mr Daniel were found guilty and sentenced to long terms of imprisonment.[15]
The problems involved in proving "anti-Soviet intent" both in literature and in
public demonstrations like those which preceded and followed the Sinyavsky-
Daniel trial further convinced Soviet authorities of the need for broader legislation limiting the right to "freedom of speech" and "freedom of assembly".
Within months of the Sinyavsky-Daniel trial, two new articles were added to
the criminal codes. In the RSFSR Criminal Code they are numbered 190-1 and
190-3.

**Article 190-1 Circulation of Fabrications Known to Be False Which Defame Soviet
State and Social System.** The systematic circulation in an oral form of
fabrications known to be false which defame the Soviet state and social
system and, likewise, the preparation or circulation in written, printed

12. Harold J. Berman, and James W. Spindler, *Soviet Criminal Law and Procedure*
(Harvard University Press, Cambridge, Massachusetts, 1972).
13. Ibid.
14. See for example G.Z. Anashkin, I.I. Karpiets and B.S. Nikiforov (editors),
*Kommentarii K Ugolovnomu Kodeksu RSFSR* (Moscow, 1971) page 168.
Hereafter this title will be cited in English: *Commentary to the RSFSR Criminal
Code* (1971).
15. For a discussion of the legal issues involved in the case against Sinyavsky and Daniel
see Harold J. Berman and James W. Spindler, *Soviet Criminal Law and Procedure*,
"Introduction", page 81, and Leopold Labedz and Max Hayward (editors), *On
Trial: The Soviet State Versus "Abram Tertz" and "Nikolai Arzhak"* (Collins-
Harvill, London, 1967)

or any other form of works of such content shall be punished by deprivation of freedom for a term not exceeding 3 years, or by correctional tasks for a term not exceeding one year, or by a gine not exceeding 100 rubles.[16]

**Article 190-3: Organization of or Active Participation in, Group Actions Which Violate Public Order.** The organization of, and, likewise, the active participation in, group actions which violate public order in a coarse manner or which are attended by clear disobedience of the legal demands of representatives of authority or which entail the violation of the work of transport or of state and social institutions or enterprises shall be punished by deprivation of freedom for a term not exceeding 3 years, or by correctional tasks for a term not exceeding one year, or by a fine not exceeding 100 rubles.[17]

These new articles differ from Articles 70 and 72 in that they carry less severe penalties than the latter. However, Articles 190-1 and 190-3 can more easily be applied because conviction under them requires no proof of "anti-Soviet intent" on the part of the defendant. The prosecution must nonetheless prove that the defendant under Article 190-1 knew that the opinions or statements he disseminated were false and slanderous.[18] This has not prevented Soviet courts from convicting many persons under Articles 190-1 and 190-3 for having communicated to other Soviet citizens criticisms of Soviet institutions or official policies. For example, five people who protested in Red Square, Moscow, in August 1968 against five Warsaw Pact countries' occupation of Czechoslovakia were each convicted under both Articles 190-1 and 190-3: the court ruled that the slogans "Down with the Occupiers", "Hands off the CSSR", "Freedom for Dubcek" and "For Your Freedom and Ours", which appeared on placards carried by the demonstrators, "represent deliberately false fabrications discrediting the Soviet State and social system."[19]

Another example of the method of application of these new articles came at the August 1967 trial of Vladimir Bukovsky, Vadim Delone and Evgeny Kushev, who were charged under Article 190-3 for having taken part in a tiny and brief demonstration in Pushkin Square, Moscow, in protest against the legislation of Articles 190-1 and 190-3. The prosecutor said in his concluding speech at the trial:

The grounds for the application of Article 190-3 are the following: Soviet citizens have the right to express dissatisfaction with certain things including actions by the authorities, but for this there exists an established order of procedure. In staging their demonstration, the accused did not follow this procedure, thereby committing a breach of the peace. The breach of the peace was gross: gross because of its impudence — impudence is shown by the fact that they criticized

16. Berman and Spindler, ibid.
17. Ibid.
18. *Commentary to the RSFSR Criminal Code* (1971), page 404.
19. Nataliya Gorbanevskaya, *Red Square at Noon* (Andre Deutsch, London, 1972), page 225. This volume includes extensive documentation on the trial. The five convicted persons were: Vladimir Dremlyuga, Vadim Delone, Larissa Bogoraz, Pavel Litvinov and Konstantin Babitsky.

existing laws and the activities of the security services, thereby under-
mining their authority. Basically, public order was violated by the
slogans.[20]
All three defendants were found guilty.

These new laws, together with Articles 70 and 72, have been applied many
times and to many persons who have expressed dissenting political views or who
have tried to exercise their constitutional right to "freedom of assembly" in an
unapproved of manner. The development of *samizdat*[21] as an alternative to
officially controlled media has been met with a large number of arrests of persons
on charges of preparation, possession or distribution of *samizdat*. Since production, possession or distribution of *samizdat per se* is not proscribed under
Soviet law, the authorities seek grounds for prosecution by attacking the contents of *samizdat* documents as "anti-Soviet" or "false and slanderous of the
Soviet state and social system".

An indication of the spirit in which this repressive campaign has been carried
out is provided in the *samizdat* transcript of the trial of Mikhail Kheifets in
September 1974. Mr Kheifets, a young Leningrad writer, was charged with
"anti-Soviet propaganda" connected with his having written an essay on the
poetry of Joseph Brodsky. In court Mr Kheifets admitted that he had circulated
a draft copy of his essay among friends with the intention of obtaining their
opinion on his essay's quality. The prosecution's reaction can be seen in the
following extract from the transcript:

| | |
|---|---|
| *Prosecutor:* | Did you yourself realize that it [your essay] was anti-Soviet? |
| *Mr Kheifets:* | Not entirely. |
| *Prosecutor:* | But was it altered? Did it remain anti-Soviet? |
| *Mr Kheifets:* | [It remained] dissenting. |
| *Prosecutor:* | But 13 persons read it! |
| *Mr Kheifets:* | Thirteen persons who were not propagandized or agitated by it! |
| *Prosecutor:* | No. Even this was anti-Soviet agitation and propaganda, and persistent at that![22] |

Mr Kheifets was found guilty of "anti-Soviet agitation and propaganda" and
sentenced to 4 years in a strict regime corrective labour camp and 2 years'
exile.

The Soviet criminal law also contains provisions restricting citizens' right to
"freedom of worship". Article 142 of the RSFSR Criminal Code reads:

> **Violation of Laws on Separation of Church and State and of Church
> and School.** The violation of laws on the separation of church and state
> and of school and church shall be punished by correctional tasks for
> a term not exceeding one year or by a fine not exceeding 50 roubles.

20. Pavel Litvinov, *The Demonstration in Pushkin Square* (Harvill Press, London, 1969)
page 77.
21. *Samizdat* (literally "self-published") writings are those which are typed and distributed
outside the official monopoly on publications.
22. The full text of this *samizdat* transcript is available in *Information Bulletin* Number
51 (Khronika Press, New York, 1974).

The same acts committed by a person previously convicted of violation of laws on the separation of church and state and of school and church, as well as organizational activity directed to the commission of such acts, shall be punished by deprivation of freedom for a term not exceeding 3 years."[23]

This law is extremely vague, and offences under it are defined only in a decree passed by the Supreme Soviet of each union republic in 1966. Among other things, the 1966 decree makes illegal the "organized and systematic" teaching of religious principles to minors.[24] It is questionable how much this decree conflicts with Article 124 of the USSR Constitution which asserts "freedom of conscience" and recognizes "freedom of religious worship and freedom of anti-religious propaganda . . . for all citizens". The 1966 decree definitely conflicts with the Convention on the Elimination of All Forms of Racial Discrimination (signed by the USSR) which asserts the right of all parents to teach their children according to their own convictions.

However, this decree is quite compatible with the USSR Fundamentals of Marriage and Family Law. Article 1 of the latter sets as a fundamental task of Soviet family law "the final elimination of harmful survivals and customs of the past in family relations", a category which includes religious education. The same Fundamentals (Article 18) also state that "parents must educate their children in the spirit of the moral code of the builders of communism". Dissenting Evangelical-Christian Baptists arguing for their right to educate their children in a religious spirit often cite the 1918 Decree on the Separation of Church from State and of School from Church, which was signed by Lenin and which stated in part: "Citizens may give or receive religious instruction privately."[25]

Article 142 of the 1960 code as amended by the 1966 decree on religious offences is used frequently against many members of the dissenting wing of the Evangelical-Christians and Baptists. Because they refused to submit to stringent restrictions imposed on religious activities in the early 1960s,[26] the dissenting Baptists (often referred to as "reform" Baptists or *Initsiativniki*) broke away from the officially-recognized Evangelical-Christian Baptist organization. Many dissenting Baptists have been imprisoned or deprived by courts of their parental rights under Article 142, mainly on charges of instructing their children in religious principles. The official attitude was succinctly stated by the prosecutor in the 1966 trial of Gennady Kryuchkov and Georgy Vins, two leading spokesmen of the dissenting Baptists:

Kryuchkov describes as heroes people who, in defiance of the law, give instruction to small children. This attitude of his towards transgressors

23. Berman and Spindler, ibid.
24. *Vedomosti Verkhovnogo Soveta RSFSR*, 1966, Number 12
25. Council of People's Commissars' Decree On the Separation of Church from State and of School from Church (20 January 1918).
26. These restrictions were established by a decree of the RSFSR Supreme Soviet dated 19 December 1962. See Gerhard Simon, *Church, State and Opposition in the USSR* (C. Hurst & Company, London, 1974) page 155. (This volume was published in German in 1970 by Manz Verlag, Munich, under the title *Die Kirchen in Russland: Berichte, Dokumente.*)

*Above:* A page from issue number 10 (1972) of the *samizdat* "Bulletin of the Council of Relatives of Imprisoned Evangelical and Christian Baptists". The page includes photos of 40 such prisoners together with addresses and brief case-histories.

25

of the law is particularly scandalous.

Kryuchkov and Vins are well aware of the ideology that dominates our society — one that has nothing in common with religion. Yet, in spite of our ideology and in spite of what is taught in the schools, they go and organize religious instruction for children.[27]

As of September 1974, 180 dissenting Baptists were serving prison sentences for religious "offences". In late 1974, Soviet officials announced to visiting representatives of the world Baptist community that 60 dissenting Baptists had been released on amnesty in the preceding two months.[28] Information emanating since then from the USSR corroborates this official statement.

Large numbers of Orthodox Christians, Pentecostalists, Jehovah's Witnesses, Buddhists, Moslems and persons of other religious persuasions are imprisoned in the USSR for religious "offences". The total number of religious prisoners is not known. However, judging from the frequency of reference to them in reports and statements by prisoners and former prisoners, religious prisoners form a substantial proportion of the total number of prisoners of conscience.

Leaders of religious groups are especially subject to imprisonment under Article 227 of the RSFSR Criminal Code (or its equivalent in other union republics). Article 227 reads:

> **Infringement of Person and Rights of Citizens Under Appearance of Performing Religious Ceremonies.** The organizing or directing of a group, the activity of which, carried on under the appearance of preaching religious beliefs and performing religious ceremonies, is connected with the causing of harm to citizens' health or with any other infringements of the person or rights of citizens, or with the inducing of citizens to refuse social activity or performance of civic duties, or with the drawing of minors into such a group, shall be punished by deprivation of freedom for a term not exceeding 5 years or by exile for a similar term with or without confiscation of property.
>
> The active participation in the activity of a group specified in paragraph one of the present article, or the systematic propaganda directed at the commission of acts specified therein, shall be punished by deprivation of freedom for a term not exceeding 3 years, or by exile for the same term, or by correctional tasks for a term not exceeding one year.
>
> *Note:* If the acts of persons stated in paragraph two of the present article, and the persons themselves, do not represent a great social danger, measures of social pressure may be applied to them.[29]

There are many cases in which the religious activities of Orthodox and Roman Catholic priests and dissenting Baptist pastors have been interpreted by investigating officials and courts so as to bring a conviction under Article 227. In

27. Cited in Michael Bourdeaux, *Faith on Trial in Russia* (Hodder and Stoughton, London, 1971) page 118.
28. *The Daily Telegraph* (London), 17 December 1974; *Le Monde* (Paris) 23 January 1975.
29. Berman and Spindler, ibid. "Measures of social pressure" consist not in penalties prescribed by the courts but in warnings, reprimands, small fines, etc., meted out by social organizations and "comrades courts".

recent times the most bizarre application of Article 227 occurred in the case of
Bidya Dandaron.[30] Mr Dandaron, born in 1914, the son of a leading Buddhist
lama, served almost 20 years in Soviet prison camps after 1937, and was rehabilitated (that is officially acknowledged to have been innocent) in 1956.
He thereupon took up his study of Buddhism and Tibetan culture and became
a recognized expert in these fields.

Living in Ulan Ude (in Buryatiya, a region with a strong Buddhist tradition).
Mr Dandaron attracted many pupils who were interested in the study of Oriental
culture. According to an anonymous *samizdat* letter to a Soviet official by colleagues of Mr Dandaron, a circle was formed based on "friendship and common
interests".[31]

In August 1972, Mr Dandaron was arrested and charged under Article 227
of the RSFSR Criminal Code. The bill of indictment accused him of leadership of a Buddhist "sect", of having led his followers in "bloody sacrifices" and
"ritual copulations", of "attempts to murder or beat former members of the
sect who had wanted to break with it", and of "contacts with foreign countries
and international Zionism".[32]

Most of these charges were dropped at Mr Dandaron's trial in Ulan Ude in
December 1972. Nonetheless, the court accepted as proven charges that the
"Dandaron group" held prayer meetings and had an illicit financial fund and that
Mr Dandaron has acted as a "guru" to the group.[33] Mr Dandaron was sentenced
to 5 years' deprivation of freedom, and died in a corrective labour colony near
Lake Baikal on 26 October 1974.[34] A number of his associates were also charged
under criminal law, submitted to psychiatric diagnoses which found them mentally
ill and consigned to psychiatric institutions.[35]

Both the RSFSR Criminal Code (Article 143, "Obstruction of Performance of
Religious Rites") and the 1966 RSFSR Supreme Soviet decree require punishment of those who interfere with citizens' exercise of their religious rights. Yet in
many places, lists are made up of believers employed in enterprises, and school
children from families of believers have been subjected to various forms of intimidation and provocation.[36] Dissenting Baptists frequently complain that they

30. Mr Dandaron's case has been described in *A Chronicle of Current Events* (Amnesty International Publications, London, 1975), Number 28, pages 24-28. *A Chronicle of Current Events* is a *samizdat* journal produced in Moscow and devoted ex- clusively to reporting violations of human rights in the Soviet Union. It has appeared on a regular basis since 1968, with an interval from October 1972 to May 1974. Amnesty International has published English translations of the *Chronicle* since 1970. On the Dandaron case see also *Religion in Communist Lands* (Keston College, Kent, England), July-October 1973, pages 43-47, and *The Observer* (London), 1 December 1974.
31. Anonymous *samizdat* letter to V.A. Kuroyedov, President of the Council for Religious Affairs attached to the Soviet Council of Ministers (15 February 1973), in *Religion in Communist Lands* (Keston College, Kent, England,) July-October 1973, page 43.
32. *A Chronicle of Current Events*, Number 28, page 24.
33. Ibid, page 25.
34. *The Observer* (London), 1 December 1974.
35. *A Chronicle of Current Events*, Number 28 page 25. See also below, Chapter VII, "Compulsory Detention in Psychiatric Hospitals".
36. See for example reportage from the Ukraine in *Bratsky Listok*, Number 1, 1974. *Bratsky Listok* ("Fraternal Leaflet") is a *samizdat* publication of the dissenting Evangelical-Christian Baptists.

suffer discrimination in employment and education (in direct violation of the 1966 decree elaborating on the content of Article 142 of the RSFSR Criminal Code). There are well-documented cases of dissenting Baptists being beaten and even shot during police actions against religious congregations. For example, Nikolai Ivanovich Loiko of Minsk was shot and badly wounded by a militia officer, Captain Pyotr Lukyanov, during a police operation against a prayer meeting in a forest near Mogilev, Belorussiya, on 2 May 1974.[37]

While both Articles 142 and 227 are regularly invoked in criminal cases against religious believers, there seems to be no such legal action against governmental and police officials guilty of specifically prohibited harassments of religious believers.

### Arrest and Detention

There are stringent regulations governing procedures for search, arrest and detention without trial. No one may be arrested without the written sanction of a procurator. Yet while an effort is made to place arrest and detention on a strictly legal basis so that allegations of arbitrariness can be refuted, well-documented instances of procedural infringements and even physical violence are frequent. Describing the arrest in October 1970 of a 19-year-old Jew from Kharkov in the Ukraine, Jonah Kolchinsky, apparently on account of his application to emigrate to Israel, *A Chronicle of Current Events* (Number 17, December 1970) reported that a

> double police-squad and a "witness" armed with a heavy object burst into the flat . . . Having cut the telephone wire, the policemen beat up Kolchinsky and arrested him. Kolchinsky was again beaten up in the car on the way to the police station. For 24 hours he was held there without food and subjected to anti-semitic insults. They shaved his head then shaved off his beard by force, and after the trial behind closed doors lasting two minutes (by one judge and a secretary) he was sent to prison for 20 days. There Kolchinsky was kept on strict regime and developed pneumonia . . . At the end of December (after six weeks' detention) Kolchinsky was released from confinement and called up into the Army.[38]

It must not be assumed that such overt brutality stems from general policy. More likely it is due to excesses by local bureaucrats and police officials. However, the possibility for violation of procedural rights of accused or suspected persons is strongly rooted in Soviet legal practice, and complaints, especially by victims who are political dissidents or religious believers, are seldom acknowledged and appear to have little or no effect.

According to law, pre-trial detention during a preliminary investigation may not under any circumstances last for more than nine months. If the investiga-

---

37. This incident was attested to by many letters from dissenting Baptists to Soviet authorities in mid-1974. See for example the "Appeal" to Soviet leaders (May 1974) by "The Christian Youth of Byelorussia", published in English in *The Samizdat Bulletin* (San Mateo, California), December 1974.
38. *A Chronicle of Current Events*, Number 17, page 67.

tion is extended beyond this limit the detainee must be released from custody pending a decision to bring him to trial or to close the case.[39] Despite this requirement, persons arrested on political charges are held for periods as long as 12 months (for example Yury Galanskov, Alexander Ginzburg, Petras Plumpa-Pluira, Povilas Petronis, Jonas Stašaitis) and even 14 months (Pyotr Yakir). Normally no attempt is made at legally justifying such violations. An exception occurred in the case of the Ukrainian mathematician Leonid Plyushch, arrested in January 1972 and not tried until January 1973. The investigator announced that the USSR Supreme Soviet has formally approved the extension of Plyushch's investigation period to one year, and that Nikolai Podgorny and Mikhail Georgadze, respectively Chairman and Secretary of the USSR Supreme Soviet Presidium, had signed the decision.[40]

Persons being held in detention pending trial can receive visitors, meet with a lawyer or correspond with "relatives or other citizens" only when the investigation officials give permission.[41] They can thus legally be held incommunicado for up to nine months after arrest.

Gabriel Superfin, a Moscow literary scholar arrested in July 1973 on a charge of "anti-Soviet agitation and propaganda", was not allowed to select a defence counsel and was obliged to study the material compiled in the course of the preliminary investigation without the assistance of a lawyer,[42] despite the provisions laid down in Articles 201 and 202 of the Code of Criminal Procedure requiring that defence counsel be present at the stage when the accused is allowed to examine his file prior to the drawing up of an indictment.

Bail is extremely rare and is unlikely to be granted in a political case. Academician Andrei Sakharov and his wife Elena Bonner offered to stand surety for mathematician Yury Shikhanovich after the latter had spent four months in detention in the autumn and winter of 1972 on a charge (under Article 70) of possessing "anti-Soviet" literature. Although eminently qualified to stand surety, Academician Sakharov was informed by KGB officials at an interview that "the KGB did not consider him an individual who satisfied the requirements made of guarantors in such cases". In the event, Mr Shikhanovich was held for a year without once being granted a meeting with his wife or even with a lawyer.[43]

## Defence Counsel

Procedures for legal defence as laid down in current Soviet legislation are generally acceptable from the human rights point of view. However their application to political cases regularly involves abuses of the rights of the accused and breaches of the Soviet law.

According to Article 46 of the RSFSR Code of Criminal Procedure, and ac-

39. RSFSR Code of Criminal Procedure, Article 97.
40. *Samizdat* "Appeal to the International Psychiatric Association (sic) and the International Lawyers' Association (sic)" by T. Khodorovich (June 1973).
41. USSR Supreme Soviet Statute "On Remand In Custody" (published in English by Progress Publishers, Moscow, 1970), Articles 12, 13.
42. *A Chronicle of Human Rights in the USSR*, (Khronika Press, New York) Number 8, pages 9-14.
43. Ibid., Number 4, pages 35-36.

cording to the corresponding codes of each of the other constituent republics of the USSR, the accused has the right to defence counsel. According to Article 48 of the RSFSR Code of Criminal Procedure, the accused can select his own defence counsel *(advokat)*, and, if he allows the investigator or court to choose his counsel, he must give consent to the selection of his counsel.

However the value of counsel to a defendant is limited by a number of factors. In all types of cases, the accused has the right to meet his counsel only on permission of the investigative officials.[44] This applies even when the accused is being held in preventive detention. Since persons can be held in preventive detention for as long as nine months, the accused may face the entire investigation without the benefit of counsel.

In political cases, other, even more serious, factors impede the effectiveness of the accused's right to counsel. All practising *advokaty* in the USSR belong to the *Kollegiya Advokatov* (Collegium of Advocates). The 1962 RSFSR statute on the tasks of the *advokaty* demands that "an *advokat* must be a model of strict and undeviating observance of Soviet laws".[45] Like their counterparts in other legal systems Soviet *advokaty* have an obligation not only to their clients but to society. However, the possibility of conflict between these obligations is compounded by the role assumed by the Communist Party of the Soviet Union in determining what constitutes the interests of society. Sixty per cent of *advokaty* are members or candidate members of the Communist Party of the Soviet Union.[46] This means that they have a dual subordination: to the law and to the party, the latter institution requiring uncompromising obedience to its rules and policies.[47]

Any *advokat* can thus be placed in the dilemma of having to choose between "strict and undeviating observance of Soviet laws" and obedience to party policy. It is quite inexpedient for an *advokat* to give precedence to any professional calling before the demands of party policy. In the cases of political defendants deemed by the party leadership to be (for example) "anti-Soviet", a communist *advokat* is constrained in his legal activity by the demands of the party. It must be added that even *advokaty* who are not members of the party are subject to similar constraints, although not of the same formal variety.

Even in the presence of these real limitations on the value of *advokaty*, the political defendant may prefer one *advokat* over another as his defence counsel. However, there exists an extra-legal system of "clearances" *(dopuski)*, according to which only an *advokat* who has a special clearance may defend in cases requiring access to "secret files", a category to which political cases belong in the USSR.[48] This placing of special trust in some *advokaty* to the exclusion of others contradicts the official position that all members of the Collegium of

44. RSFSR Code of Criminal Procedure, Article 47.
45. Statute on the Advocacy (July 1962), *Sovetskaya Iustitsia.* Numbers 15-16, 1962.
46. *Sovetskoye Gosudarstvo i Pravo*, Number 5, 1972, pages 10-19.
47. The currently effective rules of the CPSU state: "A member of the Party is obliged to observe Party and State discipline, uniformly binding for all Party members. The Party has one discipline and one law for all Communists, irrespective of their work and of the positions held by them." *(Ustav Kommunistichiskogo Partii Sovetskogo Soyuza,* Article 2.)
48. See Valery Chalidze, *To Defend These Rights: Human Rights and the Soviet Union* (Random House, New York, 1975), page 129 ff.

Advocates have the requisite moral and professional qualities, and reflects official concern that nothing upset the process by which political trials lead inexorably to conviction.

Because of the system of clearances, political defendants have sometimes been effectively deprived of the right to choose their defence counsel, the most famous example being Vladimir Bukovsky in 1972.[49]

Equally important is the fact that *advokaty* in possession of the special clearance are often reluctant to risk losing it by acting too boldly in their defence activity and merely plead for mitigation rather than seeking acquittal. Numerous cases of this have been documented. For example in the case of Valery Kukui, a Jewish would-be emigrant tried for "anti-Soviet slander" in Sverdlovsk in June 1971, defence counsel Naumov told the court that the defendant had committed no crime, but pleaded only for a reduced sentence.[50]

Some uncompromising lawyers who were too forthright in defending clients accused of politically dissident activity have lost their clearances and the right to defend in political cases (for example S. Kallistratova, D. Kaminskaya and Yu. Pozdeyev). Their examples are not encouraging for their colleagues in the Collegium of Advocates. In numerous political cases the conduct of the defence has been sluggish and unimaginative, with defence counsel often agreeing with the charges made against his client and asking merely for a lower sentence rather than for acquittal.

There have been cases of outright persecution of *advokaty* who refused to compromise in their defence of political clients. The best known such case was that of B.A. Zolotukhin, a leading Moscow lawyer who defended Alexander Ginzburg in Moscow in 1968. Mr Zolotukhin's defence was highly admired by friends of Mr Ginzburg. However, within five months Mr Zolotukhin was expelled from the party, from the presidium of the Collegium of Advocates, from his post as head of a legal consultative office and finally from the Collegium of Advocates itself. The reason given was Mr Zolotukhin's "adopting a non-party, non-Soviet line in his defence" of Ginzburg.[51] The consequence was that Mr Zolotukhin was deprived of the right to work as a defence lawyer.

Another *advokat* who has suffered a similar fate is I.S. Yezhov, who in 1973 in the Ukraine defended Alexander Feldman, a Jew convicted on apparently fabricated charges of hooliganism. Mr Yezhov has been struck off the register of the Kiev Collegium of Advocates and subjected to other forms of pressure.[52]

Finally, even vigorous defence by a sympathetic defence counsel willing to

49.    *A Chronicle of Current Events,* Number 23, page 60.
50.    Ibid., Number 21, pages 276-278.
51.    Ibid, Number 1, in Peter Reddaway, *Uncensored Russia* (London, Jonathan Cape, 1972), page 85.
52.    *Khronika Tekushchikh Sobitii (A Chronicle of Current Events)* Number 32, (Khronika Press, New York, 1974) page 48. *Khronika Tekushchikh Sobitii* is the original Russian-language version of *A Chronicle of Current Events,*, each issue of which is published in Russian by Khronika Press in New York. At the time of writing of this report, issues 32 to 35 of the *Chronicle* have not yet been published in English translation. Therefore, citations of material from these issues will be from the Russian-language publication, *Khronika Tekushchikh Sobitii.*

challenge violations of court and criminal procedure is little help in political cases.

## Trial

There has never in Amnesty International's experience been an acquittal of a political defendant in the USSR. No Soviet court trying a person charged for his political activity has rejected the prosecution's case on grounds of procedural violations committed during the investigation period or on grounds of insufficient evidence.

That such cases once begun always end in a conviction indicates that criteria other than criminal culpability are decisive. The counter-argument might be that the investigative organs do their job so thoroughly that there is no chance of mistake. However if the investigators are always correct, then the courts' decisions are irrelevant except in determination of sentence. Furthermore, the "infallibility" of investigative organs applies apparently only to "political" cases. There is a very significant incidence of acquittal in criminal cases. It is clear that in political cases the procuracy, officially the watchdog for observance of legality, steps aside on behalf of "higher" (political) considerations.

To ensure that the predetermined "guilty" verdict is arrived at in political cases, Soviet courts regularly make rulings which directly contravene the procedural norms laid down in Soviet law.

Article 111 of the Soviet Constitution states that the examination of all cases in all courts shall be open insofar as the law does not provide for exceptions. Many political trials, in fact, constitute the exceptions to this rule. Proceedings are often held effectively *in camera,* and sometimes close relatives and friends of the accused are not admitted into the courtroom — on various pretexts such as that "the public benches are fully occupied". The trial of the Ukrainian historian Valentyn Moroz was held formally *in camera* without the presence of even a specially selected audience and with no formal justification.[53]

Quite often the place, date and time of a trial are changed at the very last minute, or even after proceedings have begun. Relatives of the accused have lodged protests at what appears to be a deliberate failure to inform them. Since the creation of the unofficial Moscow Human Rights Committee[54] led by Academician Sakharov, there have been attempts by its members — chiefly Academician Sakharov — to attend political trials, but the authorities have rarely allowed them entry. Demonstrators outside court buildings at trials of dissenters are frequently handled roughly by court officials and KGB personnel, or indeed detained for hours or even days.

Inside the courtroom, the "general public", sometimes in uniform and brought in by coach, have often interrupted the proceedings with hostile comments and jeers, or, at Jewish trials, with anti-semitic remarks, or with calls

53. *A Chronicle of Current Events,* Number 17, pages 41-43.
54. The Committee of Human Rights for the USSR was formed in Moscow in November 1970. Its founding members were Academician Andrei D. Sakharov, Andrei H. Tverdokhlebov and Valery N. Chalidze, all physicists. Its goals and statutes are described in *A Chronicle of Current Events,* Number 17, pages 45-47.

for a harsher sentence. Transcripts of political trials often find their way into *samizdat,* and show that on many occasions numerous articles of the Code of Criminal Procedure have been violated.[55] Almost invariably in such trials the evidence accepted by the court has been incomplete and unfairly weighted to the disadvantage of the defendant. In many cases defence witnesses have not been allowed to give evidence. Often defence witnesses who have been called have been prevented from giving evidence other than that elicited by the prosecution. Frequently contradictions and patent falsehoods in evidence given by prosecution witnesses have been accepted by courts without challenge. In cases where the prosecution has brought in an "expert psychiatric diagnosis" recommending confinement of political defendants to a mental institution, the courts have invariably accepted such recommendations in spite of their unacceptability as objective evidence.[56]

Officially authorized publicity of political trials is extremely rare and, when it does occur, is so one-sided in presentation of the matter that one must conclude that such publicity is aimed at making propaganda rather than at elucidation of fact. For example, the trial of Sinyavsky and Daniel in 1966, the trial of Ginzburg and Galanskov in 1968, and, more recently, that of Pyotr Yakir and Victor Krasin in August 1973 were officially reported by the Soviet media in a tendentious fashion aimed at discrediting the accused men in the eyes of public opinion at home and abroad by linking them with various anti-Soviet or emigré organizations. After the trial of Yakir and Krasin, a news conference was even staged, partly for the benefit of foreign correspondents. The convicted men were officially presented, and they delivered prepared statements admitting their guilt. The event occasioned an official propaganda campaign against Western correspondents in Moscow and against the human rights movement in the USSR. *Izvestiya,* for example, quoted Mr Yakir as saying that what is often called the "democratic movement" in the USSR was only executing a program and tactics brought into the country by an "anti-Soviet" emigré organization.[57]

There are no known instances of officially-published Soviet newspapers or journals criticizing or challenging a "guilty" sentence in a political case. This is in marked contrast to the Soviet press record on non-political criminal cases, about which Soviet publications do occasionally write in defence of convicted persons on various grounds.[58] This contrast again underlines the fact that in Soviet legal practice political defendants are, to their disadvantage, treated as a separate category of "offenders".

## Penalties

Article 21 of the RSFSR Criminal Code outlines the range of punishments which may be applied for criminal offenses. They are:
> — deprivation of freedom

55. A catalogue of such procedural violations can be found in Pavel Litvinov, *The Trial of the Four* (Penguin Books, London, 1972).
56. See below, Chapter VII. "Compulsory Detention in Psychiatric Hospitals".
57. *Izvestiya,* (Moscow) 31 August 1973.
58. See Alois Hastrich, "Juristischer Alltag in der Sowjetunion", *Osteuropa* (Berlin and Stuttgart), Number 10, October 1973), pages 791-806.

- exile
- banishment
- correctional tasks without deprivation of freedom
- deprivation of the right to occupy certain offices or engage in certain activity
- fine
- dismissal from office
- imposition of the duty to make amends for harm caused
- social censure
- confiscation of property
- deprivation of military or special rank

In addition, the death penalty may be applied "as an exceptional measure" to persons convicted of any of 18 different crimes, including "treason", "espionage", "terrorist acts", a variety of economic crimes and several crimes of violence. In time of war, certain other crimes are punishable by death. As far as is known to Amnesty International, no Soviet prisoners of conscience have been executed in recent years.

Most persons convicted of political or religious "crimes" are sentenced to "deprivation of liberty": that is, to imprisonment in a prison or in a corrective labour colony. Terms of imprisonment range from one year to 15 years, the latter being the statutory maximum sentence of imprisonment. To a sentence of "deprivation of liberty" may also be added a sentence of a number of years in "exile", to be served on completion of the prison term. A person serving a sentence of exile is required to live in a location (usually small and remote) determined by administrative authorities. Although such persons may legally move freely within the determined area, they are closely supervised by local state and MVD authorities.

Occasionally persons convicted of political "crimes" are sentenced to exile instead of imprisonment. This has been so in some cases of first offenders, young defendants and female defendants. However, it is difficult to detect a coherent pattern of leniency for such persons. In February 1975, a Ukrainian court convicted Oksana Popovich of "anti-Soviet agitation and propaganda". Oksana Popovich, born in 1928, had served 10 years in labour camps for Ukrainian nationalist activities. As a result of this imprisonment she was left physically disabled. In the autumn of 1974 she was again arrested. At her trial the prosecution charged that she had distributed *samizdat* and several years earlier had collected money to pay lawyers' fees for Ukrainian political prisoners. Prior to her trial, Oksana Popovich was convalescing from surgery and restricted to crutches and was awaiting another operation. Nonetheless, she was sentenced to 8 years' imprisonment in a strict regime corrective labour colony and 5 years' exile.[59]

The courts only rarely pass a suspended sentence in a political case. The most prominent recent example of this was in February 1975 in the Leningrad trial of Vladimir Maramzin, a writer arrested in connection with his efforts to com-

---

59. See Smoloskyp Information Service Press Release, 19 April 1975, and *Khronika Tekushchikh Sobitii*, Number 34, page 23.

pile a collection of the poems of Joseph Brodsky.[60] Shortly before his trial Mr Maramzin sent a letter to the editors of *Le Monde*.[61] In it he denied that his writings had ever been political in content, and asserted that he was not "anti-Soviet" and that he had no ties with "anti-Soviet" organizations of any sort. He concluded his letter to *Le Monde* by recognizing his guilt on the charges against him. This letter of contrition was virtually identical to the confession which Mr Maramzin delivered in court. Despite the obvious contradiction between Mr Maramzin's denial of "anti-Soviet" activity of any sort and his plea of "guilty" to charges of "anti-Soviet agitation and propaganda", the court found him guilty as charged.[62] Taking into consideration the fact that Mr Maramzin had confessed, the court suspended his 5-year sentence. The sentence was atypical. The case conformed to pattern in the court's determination to produce a "guilty" verdict on whatever grounds were convenient.

Appeals against a court sentence must be lodged within seven days of the trial. In political cases, these occasionally result in a reduction of the sentence but never in an acquittal. A verdict reached at a trial conducted in the first instance by the Supreme Court of a union republic (this includes some political trials) may not be appealed, though such cases like all others may be reviewed on the initiative of a procurator if he thinks procedural violations occurred in the first hearing of the case. Reviews of political court cases are rare.

60. Also arrested in the same case was Mikhail Kheifets. See above page 23.
61. This letter was published in full in *Le Monde* (Paris), 13 February 1975.
62. Tass English-language broadcast of 21 February 1975. Transcribed and translated by British Broadcasting Corporation in *Summary of World Broadcasts*.

# Corrective Labour Legislation

The principles on which prison institutions are run in the Soviet Union are laid down in a law approved in July 1969 by the USSR Supreme Soviet and entitled Fundamentals of Corrective Labour Legislation of the USSR and the Union Republics.

This document contains 47 articles covering the main areas of concern in the organization of prisons in the USSR.

After 1969 each of the constituent union republics passed a corrective labour code embodying the principles set down in the Fundamentals and prescribing some of the details of prison operations. The codes of the different republics are identical except in minor detail. The most important in terms of this report — and the one which will be cited throughout it — is the Corrective Labour Code of the RSFSR, because it is in the Russian Soviet Federated Socialist Republic that most political prisoners are held.

Like the criminal legislation instituted at the end of the 1950s, the current Soviet corrective labour legislation represents an effort to codify changes made in official policy since the death of Stalin. The drafting and promulgation of these laws were preceded in the mid-1960s by a broad debate on the subject of penal institutions — a debate involving not only jurists and criminologists but some expression of public opinion as well. The legislation, when it came, did not meet the hopes of some Soviet jurists for a sweeping reform of the Soviet penal system. The current corrective labour legislation retains almost completely the system of theory, regulations and practices laid down in official decrees in 1954, 1958 and 1961. The most significant changes embodied in the 1969-1970 corrective labour legislation were the apparently iron-clad guarantees for the respect of legality and adherence to regulations — an apparent reaction to the anarchy which prevailed in the corrective labour system under Stalin. Unfortunately, the current legislation's commendable invocation of the rule of the law is lamentably contradicted by many aspects of contemporary practice.

*Theory*

**Purposes of Soviet Corrective Labour Legislation**[1] The purpose of corrective labour legislation shall be to effect punishment of crime with a view not only to inflicting a penalty for a committed offence but also to correcting and reforming convicted offenders in the spirit of a conscientious attitude to labour and exact observance of the laws and respect for the rules of the socialist community, preventing the commission of fresh crimes both by convicted offenders and by other persons, and also promoting the eradication of crime.

The execution of a sentence shall not aim at inflicting physical suffering or degrading human dignity.

The fundamental question in the Soviet debate on prison legislation concerned the proper blend of two features of imprisonment: the negative feature of inflicting suffering *(prichineniye stradaniya)* and the positive feature of reforming and correcting the imprisoned individual *(ispravleniye i perevospitaniye)*. The USSR Fundamentals and the union republic codes of corrective labour represent the official solution to the dilemma of reconciling humanitarian values and socialist ideals with the exigencies of the "struggle against crime".

According to Soviet criminologists, Soviet corrective labour law has long since rejected the notion that criminal punishment is a means of gaining revenge on, and retribution from, criminals. For example, the late Professor M.D. Shargorodsky, one of the most eminent Soviet legal theoreticians, ascribed retribution as a basis of punishment to all historical religions. He asserted that the maintenance of the principle of retribution and revenge is characteristic of theories and codes of punishments in capitalist societies.[2] Legislators in socialist societies, Professor Shargorodsky maintained, have rejected the principle and regard retribution "as nothing other than a contemporary form of primitive revenge."[3]

Nonetheless, even the most recent Soviet corrective labour legislation deviates from this humanitarian principle. Article 1 of the Fundamentals of Corrective Labour Legislation states: "The execution of a sentence shall not *aim at* inflicting suffering or degrading human dignity".[4] (This statement of principle appears in the corrective labour code of every union republic). The statement is frequently cited by Soviet commentators as indication of the "socialist humaneness" essential to Soviet penal legislation. Yet its curious phraseology points to a question of principle which is resolved only with difficulty in Soviet corrective labour theory. Rather than prohibiting or condemning the inflicting of suffering on prisoners or the degradation of their human dignity, Article 1 states merely that this is not the "aim" of the execution of punishment in the USSR. Nowhere in the Fundamentals or union republic codes of corrective labour law are such actions expressly prohibited.

1.  Fundamentals of Corrective Labour Legislation of the USSR and the Union Republics (1969), Article 1.
2.  M.D. Shargorodsky, *Nakazaniye, Ego Tseli i Effektivnost'* (Moscow, 1973), page 24-25.
3.  Ibid, page 26.
4.  Emphasis supplied by *A.I.*

The official explanation for this apparent anomaly is that punishment by definition is characterized by some degree of suffering, both physical and moral.[5] Furthermore, the element of suffering in deprivation of liberty (and other forms of punishment) is officially regarded as a necessary deterrent, both for the individual prisoner and for "unstable" elements of the population who might be tempted by crime. Therefore, while Soviet literature on penal policy features frequent warnings against infliction of unnecessary suffering on prisoners, official policy is also characterized by prohibition of undue mildness in the treatment of prisoners.[6]

That Soviet corrective labour legislation and theory have not rejected outright the regularized infliction of suffering on prisoners is not merely a matter of criminological principle, but is of central importance in evaluating Soviet prison conditions in terms of human rights considerations.

The most clear expression of the purely punitive aspect of the Soviet corrective labour system is that official policy makes mandatory that prisoners should be kept in a state of permanent hunger. The RSFSR Corrective Labour Code legalizes the providing of prisoners with only that amount of food which is biologically necessary:

> Convicted persons shall receive food providing the normal functioning *[zhiznedeyatelnost]* of the human organism.[7]

A comparison of this legal norm with Article 20 of the United Nations Standard Minimum Rules for the Treatment of Prisoners is instructive:

> Every prisoner shall be provided by the administration at the usual hours with food of nutritional value adequate for the health and strength, of wholesome quality and well prepared and served.

The punitive motivation for the Soviet legal norm that prisoners should receive only the biologically necessary minimum quantity of food is explained in the following remarkable passage which appears in a textbook approved by the USSR Ministry of Internal Affairs (MVD), the ministry charged with administration of corrective labour institutions:

> Non-supply of the physiologically demanded minimum norms of food and material provisions . . . inflicts physical suffering and leads to the emaciation *[istoshcheniye]* of the organism, to illness and, finally, to the biological impoverishment of the person. *The everyday material maintenance of convicted persons who observe the demands of the regime is carried out within the physiologically necessary limits . . .* Proceeding from the punitive content of the punishment and the necessity of using it in order to obtain the goals of public deterrence and corrective education, *Soviet corrective labour legislation to a certain extent utilizes the daily material maintenance of prisoners as*

5.  N.A. Struchkov and V.A. Kirin (editors), *Kommentariik Osnovam Ispravitel'no Trudovogo Zakonodatelstva SSSR i Soyusnyhk Respublik* (Moscow, 1972) page 33. Henceforth this title will be referred to in English: *Commentary to the Fundamentals of Corrective Labour Legislation of the USSR and Union Republics* (1972).
6.  See for example V. Bolysov, "Utilize All Means of Procuracy Supervision", in *Sotsialisticheskaya Zakonnost* (Moscow), March 1975.
7.  RSFSR Corrective Labour Code, Article 56.

*a means of gaining the goals established in Article 20* of the Fundamentals of Corrective Labour Legislation of the USSR and Union Republics.[8]

The requirement that only those prisoners "who observe the demands of the
regime" shall be fed "within the physiologically necessary limits" has as a corol-
lary a reduction in food rations for prisoners who refuse to work, who "deliberately" do not fulfil their work production norms, or who are put into a punishment
cell for violations of discipline.[9] Inmates of prisons are to be fed less than prisoners held in corrective labour colonies.[10] Although in principle all prisoners in
corrective labour colonies are to be fed according to a single norm no matter
on what regime they are kept,[11] in practice successively more severe regimes
entail successive reductions in rations.[12]

This reprehensible policy of legally-prescribed hunger for all prisoners will be
discussed at greater length below. The policy is mentioned in the part of this
report dealing with the Soviet corrective labour legislation *per se,* because it
and other *purely punitive* attributes of the Soviet prison system put into per-
spective the claim that the infliction of suffering "is not a goal" of the Soviet
criminal and corrective labour law. While it is officially claimed that Soviet
penal law and policy is so characterized by "humaneness" that, by comparison,
non-socialist legal systems are primitively barbaric, the very legislation governing the Soviet prison system includes provisions making the infliction of suffering mandatory. In this respect, Soviet corrective labour legislation is not qualita-
tively different from the legislation it replaced: that which existed during the
last 20 years of the Stalin era.

On a related and ostensibly more positive issue, the current Soviet corrective
labour legislation abides by long-established Soviet tradition: the assertion that
a primary goal of the corrective labour system is the "correction and re-education" of convicted persons. This principle has been affirmed by the authors of
Soviet criminal and penal legislation throughout the existence of the Soviet
state. However, the earlier prison codes (1924 and 1933) recognized a distinction
between members of the working class whose crimes did not fundamentally
threaten the new state, and members or adherents of the "enemy classes" who
were imprisoned for actions having political significance. Under this system,
only common law criminals were to be reformed: political prisoners were regarded as not being susceptible to reform.

The present corrective labour legislation does not formally recognize this
distinction, and calls for the "reform and re-education" of all prisoners. However, by calling for more rigorous measures against "especially dangerous state
criminals", the current corrective labour legislation still implicitly singles out
political prisoners for distinctive treatment.

The official Soviet viewpoint on the treatment of prisoners is influenced pro-
foundly by the Marxist-materialist tenet that the behaviour and attitudes of
persons is determined in large measure by the objective circumstances under

8.  *Ispravitel'no Trudovoye Pravo* (Moscow, 1971), pages 323-324. Emphasis supplied
    by *A.I.*
9.  Ibid, page 326.
10. Ibid.
11. Ibid, page 325.
12. See, for example, *Khronika Tekushchikh Sobitii,* Number 33, page 9.

which they are found and the subjective influences to which they are exposed. On the basis of this undertaking, it is maintained, Soviet corrective labour institutions are charged with the task of devising and implementing a scientifically sound program for the "correction and re-education" of prisoners, the goal being that set down in Article 20 of the Fundamentals of Criminal Legislation of the USSR and Union Republics, which states in part:

> Punishment is not only chastisement for the crime committed but also has as a goal the correction and re-education of convicted persons in the spirit of an honest attitude toward work, exact compliance with the laws, respect for the rules of socialist public life . . .

This conviction brings to Soviet corrective labour legislation and theory a spirit of optimism and confidence that in the USSR imprisonment is of positive value to the prisoner rather than being mere punishment for violation of the law. However there exist among Soviet jurists and criminologists many differences of opinion as to what can be expected from practical application of the principle that prisoners can and should be "corrected" and "re-educated". For example, A.Y. Natashev and N.A. Struchkov, writing in 1967, shared the opinion

> that we can speak of correction and re-education of a convicted person only when he has become a useful member of society, that is, when he has been corrected in a moral sense and not simply ceased to commit violations out of fear of being held to account.[13]

Natashev and Struchkov went still further:

> In other words, correction and re-education must give one result: the person who has served his sentence must no longer be dangerous for society, and more, he must be able to be only of use to society.[14]

M.D. Shargorodsky rejected this fundamentalist approach as an "idealization" of the goals of punishment:

> . . . the educational tasks of punishment are gained when the law-breaker, after completing his sentence, no longer commits crimes. The position of those authors who demand the changing of the guilty person's consciousness in a moral sense (so-called moral correction) go beyond the limits of the narrow tasks which must stand before punishment in criminal law. The general task of educating a person to be a conscious citizen of a socialist society, of educating a person morally, is far from always achieved successfully even in the conditions of a normal family, school or collective; it is all the more utopian to assign such a task to measures of criminal punishment . . . where conditions are considerably more difficult for education so broad in its moral aspect.[15]

The current corrective labour legislation reflects the more radical of the two views just described regarding the desirable and expectable degree of "correction"

13. A.Y. Natashev and N.A. Struchkov, *Osnovy Teorii Ispravitel'no-Trudovogo Prava* (Moscow, 1967), page 25.
14. Ibid.
5. Shargorodsky, ibid, page 32.

of imprisoned persons. Article 30 of the Fundamentals of Corrective Labour Legislation of the USSR and the Union Republics sets as a goal "enhancing the consciousness, raising the cultural level and developing the positive initiative of the convicted persons".

The view that prisoners can and should be reformed in a fundamental way is emphasized in the *Commentary to the Fundamentals of Corrective Labour Legislation of the USSR and the Union Republics,* an authoritative volume intended as a practical guide for several categories of officials involved in corrective labour practice. According to this *Commentary,* an intensive effort to reform persons convicted for violations of criminal law is required because of the character traits common to such persons.

> Re-education of persons who have committed violations of the law is a most complicated and important task, inasmuch as exactly persons in this category as a rule have the most tenacious anti-social views and habits and a lower consciousness than other citizens.[16]

For correct fulfilment of this task, it is necessary that all individual prisoners be subjected to the most intimate scrutiny by the administrations of corrective labour institutions, according to the same official source:

> Workers of corrective labour institutions who are implementing individual educational work with condemned persons must strive to study better the personality of the convict, to find the negative qualities of his character, the weakness and gaps in his education which led him to commission of a crime, systematically to scrutinize his behaviour in the places of deprivation of freedom, to study his moral qualities, his attitude to work and to study, to the fulfilment of his social obligations, etc. All this is necessary so as to choose for the convicted person such means of individual education which will most effectively influence him and facilitate his correction and re-education.[17]

The means employed to "correct" and re-educate prisoners are labour and various forms of educational activity. Labour and some forms of moral-political education are compulsory for prisoners. Because the "program" for each prisoner varies according to such factors as the type of sentence he is serving, the "production profile" of the particular corrective labour institution and the institution's assessment of his character and need for correction, the administration of each corrective labour institution is given much latitude in deciding the nature of the effort required to reform each prisoner.

On the one hand, this situation deviates from the officially-proclaimed principle that prisons shall be highly regulated so as to prevent violations of "socialist legality" by administrators or prisoners alike. On the other hand, prison administrations have been provided by law with a mechanism which, however well-intended, can be and is used to "degrade the human dignity" of prisoners in contravention of Article 1 of the Fundamentals of Corrective Labour Legislation. This is particularly true with respect to prisoners whose "crimes" were motivated by the promptings of conscience.

16. *Commentary to the Fundamentals of Corrective Labour Legislation of the USSR and the Union Republics* (1972), page 112.
17. Ibid, page 113.

The subjection of such prisoners to the demand that they change their views represents an effort not to remove any criminal impulses, but to force them to recant their views on intellectual and moral, political and religious questions. Since the "correction" and "re-education" of prisoners is in practice tied in with a broad variety of punitive measures which can be applied both in corrective labour institutions and after release, prisoners of conscience are, in fact, faced with a degrading form of blackmail.

## Socialist Legality

The drafting of the present Soviet corrective labour laws was in response to the absence of such legislation prior to 1969. The last prison code to have been approved in the USSR was the RSFSR Corrective Labour Code of 1933. It is generally recognized that by the end of the Stalin era this code (and other union republic corrective labour codes) no longer applied. The majority of its provisions had been made obsolete or superseded by new regulations.[18] Most of these other regulations were in the form of departmental instructions issued by the NKVD or MVD.[19] In other words, the law had been superseded by a series of administrative decisions issued by various non-accountable security chiefs. This situation was characteristic of the anarchy which prevailed throughout the last 20 years of Stalin's life — anarchy which pervaded many areas of Soviet life but which was nowhere so endemic as in the relations between police organs and citizens, prison administrators and prisoners.

The years since 1953 have been marked by efforts to restore formal legality and order to the corrective labour system. The 1969 Fundamentals represent an effort to re-establish the unchallengeable and binding authority of corrective labour legislation over the operation of the penal system. The union republic corrective labour codes are intended to strengthen the binding character of the All-Union Fundamentals by providing "the fullest possible regulation of the corrective labour rules".[20]

According to Article 8 of the Fundamentals of Corrective Labour Legislation of the USSR and the Union Republics, all prisoners enjoy "the rights established by the law for the citizens of the USSR". The *Commentary to the Fundamentals of Corrective Labour Legislation of the USSR and the Union Republics* elaborates that prisoners cannot exercise all rights of Soviet citizens. Political prisoners, especially those imprisoned on charges involving the circulation of *samizdat* or participation in "anti-Soviet demonstrations", might well greet with derision the acknowledgement that prisoners cannot exercise such citizens' rights as the right to have "their own press organs" or the right to hold "processions, demonstrations and meetings".[21] In the Soviet literature on the subject, we can find no clarification as to the right of prisoners to enjoy "freedom of religious worship", a right guaranteed by Article 24 of the Soviet Constitution. There have been many cases in which this right has been denied to prisoners, especially

18. Ibid, page 5.
19. Ibid, page 5. The NKVD (People's Commissariat of Internal Affairs) was renamed the Ministry of Internal Affairs (MVD) in 1946. Then as now this state organ administers the corrective labour system in the USSR.
20. Ibid, page 23.
21. Ibid, page 40.

prisoners imprisoned on account of their religious activities.

Nonetheless, the principle is legally established that prisoners are "subjects possessing defined rights and obligations",[22] and that consequently the treatment of prisoners must be in accordance with legal definitions of their rights and obligations. Despite the strict limitations on the publication of critical descriptions of the operation of corrective labour institutions, Soviet jurists and criminologists have on numerous occasions revealed their awareness of the potential which exists for arbitrariness and perpetration of abuses against prisoners within such institutions in the USSR.[23] This recognition is reflected in numerous statements in officially-published Soviet literature on the subject condemning violations of "socialist legality" by prison administrations.

> Instances of illegality and arbitrariness, intolerable in any conditions of
> our activity, are of even greater public danger in places of deprivation
> of freedom.[24]

This attitude is based in part on the perception that lawlessness by corrective labour officials is not conducive to development of respect for law on the part of convicted persons.

Soviet corrective labour legislation has established several mechanisms for ensuring that legal norms are respected by officials and prisoners alike. Most important is the procuracy, whose approval is required for many types of decisions made by the MVD and by the corrective labour administrations, and who "are obliged to take measures in good time to prevent and eliminate any breaches of the law from whomsoever they emanate and to bring the guilty to account".[25] An important role in this respect is assigned also to public "supervisory commissions", which have sweeping authority to investigate conditions in all corrective labour institutions.[26]

Yet for all the formal legislative guarantees of this sort, the operation of the Soviet corrective labour system is characterized by flagrant and regular violations and deviations from the law. Allegations of lawlessness on the part of administrators appear constantly in the only accounts available to us of conditions in Soviet prisons and colonies: *samizdat* appeals and statements by prisoners and former prisoners.

One cannot ignore the fact that the hopes of many Soviet jurists that the current corrective labour legislation would provide iron-clad guarantees of respect for the law have been betrayed, and on several levels.

While accepting the principle that the corrective labour laws should provide strict and thorough regulation of the operations of places of imprisonment, Soviet legislators have retained the view that many decisions cannot be made according to regulations but must be governed by considerations of expediency. Consequently, in many areas of decision-making, the corrective labour laws

22. Natashev and Struchkov, ibid, pages 119-120.
23. See for example V. Bolysov, "Utilize All Means of Procuracy Supervision", in *Sotsialisticheskaya Zakonnost* (Moscow) March 1975.
24. Natashev and Struchkov, ibid, page 56.
25. Fundamentals of Corrective Labour Legislation of the USSR and Union Republics, Article 10.
26. RSFSR Corrective Labour Code, Article 110; *Commentary to the Fundamentals of Corrective Labour Legislation of the USSR and Union Republics* (1972) pages 44-45.

44

provide only vague declarations of principle. Much is left to the discretion of those charged with operation of the corrective labour system.

Thus, the norms for feeding prisoners are established by the USSR Council of Ministers.[27] The USSR Ministry of Internal Affairs (MVD), in collaboration with the Ministry of Health, defines the system of medical care for prisoners:[28] only the broadest guidelines are established by the legislation. The MVD also issues numerous regulations and instructions specifying details of the operations of corrective labour institutions. The administrations of individual corrective labour institutions are given much latitude in deciding details of the educational program[29] and work program[30] of prisoners under their authority. The administrations also have the authority to apply at their own discretion a wide variety of punishments, without consulting any higher or outside authority. Among such punishments are deprivation of the prisoner's next family visit and deprivation of the prisoner's right to spend the meagre sum allowed for purchase of supplementary food.[31]

The administration's application of some punishments, such as placing a prisoner in a punishment cell, requires the approval of the public "supervisory commission" operating in the district.[32] Certainly in the case of political prisoners such consent is a mere formality. We know of no case where an administration's decision to punish a political prisoner by placing him in a "punishment isolation cell" or "punishment cell" has been turned down by a supervisory commission.

Prisoners in colonies and prisons have said that the regulations on display in every penal institution are merely the basic principles, together with information about meal-times, work-shift hours or production norms. Prisoners are not allowed to consult the special directives and decrees which regulate the details of prison and colony life (such as the Ministry of the Interior's Instruction Number 020 of 14 January 1972, many of whose provisions are in direct conflict with the Fundamentals of Corrective Labour Legislation).[33] Nevertheless, prison and colony administrative personnel continually refer to these directives when charging prisoners with infringements of the rules.

The fact that prison administrators do not feel constrained in their actions by the corrective labour legislation has been illustrated many times and in many ways. For example, in June 1974 Major Pimenov, head of Perm corrective labour colony VS 389/35, told hunger-striking political prisoners that he had "absolute authority".[34]

The procuracy, entrusted with ensuring the observance of legality in the camps and the conformance of some kinds of administrative regulations (by the MVD and the administrations of individual corrective labour institutions) to

27.   RSFSR Corrective Labour Code, Article 56.
28.   Ibid. Article 57.
29.   Ibid, Article 44.
30.   Ibid, Article 37.
31.   Ibid, Article 53.
32.   Ibid, Article 54.
33.   See below, pages 79, 83, 84
34.   "A Statement from the Psychiatrist Semyon Gluzman, a Political Prisoner",
      A Chronicle of Human Rights in the USSR (New York), Number 10, 1974, page 39.

written law, does not in practice possess the autonomy necessary for the literal execution of this task. Despite its great legal authority the procuracy almost invariably seems incapable of challenging the decisions of the MVD or of the MVD officials administering prisons and colonies.

## Categories of Imprisonment

The corrective labour legislation regulates application of the following kinds of punishment laid down by courts: deprivation of liberty, exile, restricted residence, corrective labour without deprivation of liberty. In this report only "deprivation of liberty" will be discussed.

In the Soviet Union, there are two basic types of places of imprisonment: corrective labour colonies and prisons.[35] Both are administered by the MVD. The corrective labour colony is officially regarded as the best type of institution of imprisonment, because (theoretically) it gives maximum emphasis to correction and re-education of prisoners.[36] The basic distinction between colonies and prisons is that the former are less severe than the latter. Prisons, by law, are intended to exercise a greater punitive role than colonies. However, both types of institutions are intended to punish as well as to "correct" and "re-educate". In passing sentence, courts specify in which type of institution a prisoner is to serve his sentence. A person can be sentenced to a term in prison, followed by a term in a corrective labour colony and a period of internal exile.

### a) Corrective Labour Colonies

In official terminology, the word "colony" *(koloniya)* has completely replaced the word "camp" *(lager)*. Nevertheless, prisoners almost always use the term "camp", signifying their attitude that the traditional character of the camps remains unchanged. Sentences passed in court stipulate not only the type of institution (colony or prison) to which a prisoner is to be sent, but also the type of "regime" *(rezhim)* under which, he is to be kept. There are four grades of colony regime regulating the conditions of imprisonment. They are, in order of increasing severity: ordinary *(obshchi)*, intensified *(usilenny)*, strict *(strogi)* and special *(osoby)*. The regimes differ from one another in the degree of punishment each inflicts upon the prisoner. Each entails a progressive reduction in prisoners' rights to visits, receiving of correspondence, supplementary food purchases, etc. The type and amount of work required of a prisoner varies according to his regime. Prisoners held under "special regime" are kept in cells.

The most striking difference between regimes is in diet. This is not required by corrective labour law: such law specifies that food rations shall be dependent in part on prisoners' attitudes to work but does not relate the quantity of food given to prisoners to the type of regime. Nonetheless, extra-legislative regulations stipulate that food rations shall vary according to type of regime. Stricter regimes further reduce food rations by lowering prisoners' allowed expenditure on supplementary food products.

35. Another type of imprisonment is confinement to a mental institution. This is not treated in the Soviet corrective labour legislation and will be dealt with separately in this report.

36. *Commentary to the Fundamentals of Corrective Labour Legislation of the USSR and Union Republics* (1972), page 6.

46

## b) Prisons

A sentence to a term in prison is the most severe form of deprivation of liberty. Inmates of prisons receive less food than do inmates of colonies, and their rights are subject to further severe restrictions. Whereas in corrective labour colonies prisoners (except those on special regime or those sent to punishment cells) are housed communally, persons serving their sentence in prisons are kept in cells. Generally, prison cells are shared by more than one prisoner, and the law stipulates that a prisoner cannot be placed in solitary confinement as a disciplinary measure.[37] However, prisoners can be put in solitary confinement at their own request or if the administration decides this to be necessary.[38] The grounds for placing a prisoner in solitary confinement in a prison are not defined by law, and application of this measure is left to the discretion of the prison administration. Although in such cases the prison administration is required to obtain the approval of the procurator,[39] granting such approval is likely to be a formality, especially when the prisoner concerned is a political prisoner. Thus, solitary confinement is liable to be used as a means of punishment or of revenge against recalcitrant prisoners.

A famous and most disturbing example of this abuse is the treatment received by Valentyn Moroz, a Ukrainian historian serving a long sentence in Vladimir prison for "anti-Soviet agitation and propaganda".[40] In 1972, Mr Moroz was placed in a cell with two violent criminal prisoners. They tormented him for two weeks by taking turns depriving him of sleep, and finally stabbed him in th stomach. Consequently, Mr Moroz was placed in solitary confinement, ostensib for his own protection, although there are many non-violent prisoners in Vladimir prison with whom Mr Moroz could have been lodged. In July 1974, after almost two years in solitary confinement, Mr Moroz, believing he was going insane, declared a hunger strike "to the death" in an effort to obtain transfer fror the prison to a colony. It is indicative of the conditions to which he was subjected that, after having spent almost nine full years in Soviet colonies and prisons in which hunger is a permanent feature of life, Mr Moroz felt compelled to resort to this hunger strike to obtain such a limited goal.

Mr Moroz continued his hunger strike for five months, being kept alive by forced feeding. In late November 1974 he wrote to his wife that he had begun again to take food after an official promise that he would be lodged in a cell shared by another political prisoner.[41]

There are two types of regime in prisons: "ordinary" and "strict". Prisoners on ordinary regime in prisons can spend three roubles per month on supplementary food purchases, have two short visits from outside each year, receive three packets of note paper and woollens each year and send one letter per

37. *Commentary to the Fundamentals of Corrective Labour Legislation of the USSR and Union Republics* (1972), page 86
38. Ibid, page 86.
39. RSFSR Corrective Labour Code, Article 86.
40. See *Khronika Tekushchikh Sobitii*, Number 33, pages 55-58.
41. Reuter news agency dispatch, 10 December 1974.

month. The "exercise period" allowed prisoners on ordinary regime is one hour per day. For prisoners on strict regime, these rights are further restricted. According to the law no prison inmate can be kept on strict regime for more than six consecutive months.

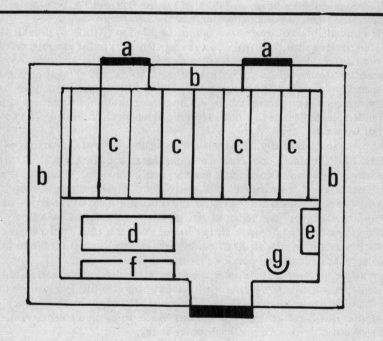

Key
a  Windows
b  Walls
c  Two-tier bunks
d  Table
e  Hanging cupboard
f  Bench
g  Slop-bucket

**Plan of a cell in special regime colony ZhKh 385-1 in the Mordovian ASSR. The plan was sketched by prisoner Boris Penson in 1974.**

## Location of Colonies and Prisons and Number of Prisoners of Conscience

Since official penal statistics are classified as state secrets, it is difficult to say how many penal institutions exist and exactly where and how they are distributed in the USSR. Amnesty International has the names, and in most cases the precise postal codes and addresses, of more than 330 prisons and labour colonies known to accommodate or to have accommodated political prisoners in recent years. Of these, more than 180 prisons and colonies are located in the RSFSR (including the area around Perm in the Urals and the Mordovian Autonomous Republic, both of which have high concentrations of political prisoners); more than 60 are in the Ukraine; and the remaining 80 or 90 are distributed throughout the other republics in areas as far afield as the Baltic coast, Belorussia, Moldavia, the Chinese border and the Central Asian republics.

The Fundamentals of Corrective Labour Legislation (Article 6) provide that convicted persons shall, "as a rule", serve their sentence in the republic on whose territory they resided prior to arrest or were convicted.

Exceptions to the rule are previous offenders, aliens, and persons convicted of "especially dangerous crimes against the state".[42] Such people may be "sent to serve sentence in corrective labour institutions set aside for these categories of offenders, regardless of the union republic in which they resided prior to arrest or were convicted".[43]

The category "especially dangerous crimes against the state" (Articles 64-73 in the RSFSR Criminal Code) embraces a number of specifically political articles under which prisoners of conscience are frequently convicted: "treason", "anti-Soviet agitation and propaganda" and "anti-Soviet" organizational activity. Many prisoners of conscience convicted under other articles of the law — such as "anti-Soviet slander" and religious articles — are not deterred by a first criminal conviction but persist in proscribed activities. If convicted a second time such persons are classified as "recidivists", and they too are liable to be sent to serve sentence in a republic other than their native one.

In practice, persons in these categories are almost always transported to serve sentence in corrective labour institutions in the RSFSR. For citizens of other than Russian nationality (Balts, Ukrainians, Uzbeks, Armenians, etc) this imposes disadvantages and deprivations which were foreseen and warned against by Soviet jurists. One official source states:

> It is fully understandable that the nearer a prisoner is located to the place of residence of his relatives the greater will be his possibility to utilize his right to meetings with them.[44]

The same authority recognizes that imprisonment in a distant place increases the punitive element of a sentence because the prisoner "must live and work in climatic conditions to which he is unaccustomed and face difficulties in the exercise of a number of rights".[45]

42. Fundamentals of Corrective Labour Legislation of the USSR and Union Republics, Article 6.
43. Ibid.
44. *Commentary to the Fundamentals of Corrective Labour Legislation of the USSR and Union Republics* (1972), page 30.
45. Ibid, pages 30-31.

In RSFSR colonies and prisons, Russian is *de facto* the language used in communications of all kinds between administrators and prisoners. There are provisions for the use of interpreters, which would tend to suggest that the language problem is officially recognized and multi-lingualism tolerated. However, cases have been recorded of prisoners being reprimanded or even punished for speaking a language other than Russian in colonies on the territory of the Russian Republic.[46] This is true of political prisoners from, for instance, the Ukraine. Many of them have been sentenced for their so-called "nationalist" views, which normally consist of the advocacy, on principle, of Ukrainian culture and language and resistance to what they regard as an official policy of Russification in their republic. In the colonies and prisons, their correspondence in Ukrainian is often confiscated for official translation, or they are asked to re-write letters *in Russian*.[47] Visists may be terminated if conversation is not in Russian. The same applies to prisoners who use Hebrew or Baltic languages.

This practice of placing prisoners in institutions located in remote parts of the RSFSR, including Mordovia and Perm, makes it extremely difficult for many families to take advantage of the already highly restricted visiting privileges. Cases have often been reported of families being unable to meet the costs of visiting imprisoned relatives.

The main concentrations of political prisoners who have committed "especially dangerous state crimes" or who are "second offenders" are in the complexes of colonies in the Mordovian Autonomous Soviet Socialist Republic some 450 kilometers south of Moscow and in Perm region.

There are many colonies in the Mordovian complex. "Especially dangerous" and "recidivist" political prisoners there are concentrated in colonies ZhKh 385/1, /3, /17 and /19. Colony 1 is a special regime colony; colony 3 holds most female political prisoners and female second offenders against laws on religion. (Twenty-two of the 300 women imprisoned there as of December 1974 were political or religious prisoners.[48] These four and a number of other colonies collectively form the "Dubrovlag" sub-complex, with the institutional acronym ZhKh 385.

The Perm complex (VS 389) is located in Chusovskoi district (some 1,200 kilometers east of Moscow) in the Perm region. Political prisoners in Perm are held in colonies 35 and 36. According to issue number 33 of *A Chronicle of Current Events* each of these two colonies holds between 200 and 250 prisoners. In addition, a third colony of the same size is being built with convict labour in the vicinity.[49]

In late 1974, four members of the Moscow "Initiative Group for the Defence

46. See for example "A Perm Camp", an anonymous report from within a colony in the Chusovskoi district in Perm province; undated, but apparently written in the autumn of 1973. Published in English in *Samizdat Bulletin* (San Mateo, California), April 1974.
47. See for example the memoir of ex-prisoner Anatoly Radygin, "Life in the Mordovian Concentration Camps", published in English by Ukrainisches Institut für Bildungspolitik (Munich, 1974) and "The Journal of a Month-Long Hunger Strike" (1974), in *A Chronicle of Human Rights in the USSR* (Khronika Press, New York), Number 10.
48. *Khronika Tekushchikh Sobitii*, Number 33, pages 17-19.
49. Ibid, page 20.

of Human Rights in the USSR" estimated that there are "around a thousand" political and religious prisoners in the Mordovian and Perm colonies.[50]

The only Soviet prison on which Amnesty International has detailed information is also in the RSFSR.[51] Vladimir prison is located in the ancient city of the same name, 175 kilometers east of Moscow. It is reserved for prisoners deemed to be the most dangerous, including political prisoners transferred there from colonies on charges of violation of colony regulations. In 1974, a former political inmate estimated that of approximately 1,500 inmates of Vladimir prison, about 35 were political prisoners.[52] Since this estimate was made, a number of political prisoners have been transferred to Vladimir prison from corrective labour colonies, bringing the probable total of prisoners of conscience in Vladimir to around 50.

It must be emphasized that while most is known about prisoners of conscience in Mordovia, Perm and Vladimir, many prisoners of conscience are held elsewhere in the USSR. First offenders convicted of (for example) "anti-Soviet slander" or religious offences may be held in less well-known colonies in the RSFSR (especially in the far east) or in colonies in their union republics. This far-flung quality of political imprisonment in the USSR is one factor which makes it extremely difficult to gather up-to-date information and statistics on prisoners of conscience and to estimate numbers.

The authorities do not publish statistics on the number of prisoners in the USSR. Since they do not even make reference to political or religious prisoners as such, one can only estimate the number of Soviet prisoners of conscience.

Any such estimate of their number among the total prison population must be made with reference to the historical background of politically-motivated imprisonment in the USSR. The enormous dimension of this phenomenon is one expression of the violence which has marked much of the history of the Soviet state. Within two generations the Soviet people have experienced two revolutions, a protracted civil war and a foreign war costing the lives of 20 million Soviet citizens. The country's economic structure has been transformed by massive compulsory collectivization of farmland and by periods of extremely rapid industrialization. Whole nations have seceded from the defunct pre-revolutionary Russian empire and later acceded one way or another to the Soviet state.

During each of these developments, large parts of the affected population groups have withheld their consent from official decisions. Official policy has been that where consent was lacking, coercion was necessary to enforce the rapid radical changes decreed by governmental bodies.

Within the Communist Party of the Soviet Union and government, regular purges were conducted until the early 1950s, each being intended to eradicate numerous individuals who were purportedly working against some part of the

50.    *Samizdat* "Statement of the Initiative Group for the Defence of Human Rights in the USSR", 30 October 1974.

51.    There is much documentation on KGB investigation prisons, which exist in every major city in the USSR. These are not formally part of the corrective labour system and prisoners do not serve sentence in them.

52.    Boris Shilkrot, "Bericht aus Vladimir", *Allgemeine Jüdische Wochenzeitung*, 30 August 1974.

leadership's policies. Among the population at large, huge numbers of people were swept into the labour camps for real or imagined opposition to official decisions related to such spheres of life as the economy, religion, nationalities, policy and intellectual activity.

Repression was institutionalized in the law in the form of the doctrine that the political interests of the Soviet state took precedence over the letter of the law and that the law itself could be dispensed with (for example by the NKVD special boards) wherever the state's interests were deemed to be threatened. Large-scale repression was further facilitated by the inclusion in the law[53] of such "catch-all" clauses as Article 7 which eliminated the commission of a crime as a necessary precondition for obtaining a criminal conviction, Article 16 which allowed conviction of a person under an article proscribing an action similar to but not identical to the action he had committed, and Article 58 which defined the widest range of actions as "counter-revolutionary activity".

Soviet authorities have condemned some of these massive abuses of authority, but only with reference to the late-Stalin period and usually with emphasis on inner-party purges. Official Soviet sources do not deal with the dimensions of political imprisonment even prior to 1953. Unofficial estimates of the number of political prisoners at the time of Stalin's death invariably range upwards from a million.

In the mid-1950s, huge numbers of political prisoners were freed from prisons and colonies and officially "rehabilitated": that is, it was officially recognized that they had been wrongfully imprisoned. No official sources have revealed the numbers of persons so released. However one semi-official indication of the number of persons amnestied was made in 1957 by P.I. Kudryavtsev, then Deputy Procurator-General of the USSR, in a conversation with the American legal scholar Harold J.Berman. Mr Kudryavtsev told Mr Berman that two-thirds of the labour camps had been abolished and that a similar proportion of the prison population had been released between 1953 and 1957.[54] Since Mr Kudryavtsev gave three million as the prison population in 1953, he implied that two million prisoners had been amnestied, a large proportion of these being political prisoners.[55]

An estimate of the present number of prisoners of conscience is complicated by the fact that many political prisoners were not released in the post-Stalin amnesties. There are regular reports referring to political prisoners (and even military prisoners) confined before 1953 who are still being held in remote Soviet prison institutions. Many persons condemned on political charges to 25-year prison sentences during the last years of Stalin's life, or even after, were not amnestied and did not even obtain reduction in their sentences when in the late 1950s the maximum sentence of imprisonment was reduced to 15 years. Information on most such persons cannot be found in the available *samizdat* materials and it is difficult to estimate their number.

53.  Here, the 1926 RSFSR Criminal Code.
54.  Harold J. Berman, "Soviet Law Reform — Dateline Moscow 1957", *Yale Law Journal*, Volume LXVI, Number 8, pages 1194-1196.
55.  Ibid.

52

*Above:* Anatoly Marchenko.　　　　　　*Above:* Valentyn Moroz

Likewise, as was mentioned above, it is difficult to calculate the number of prisoners of conscience held in remote and obscure colonies which are only vaguely reported about in *samizdat* documents.

Valery Chalidze, a former "legal expert" of the Moscow Human Rights Committee who was deprived of his Soviet citizenship in 1972, has estimated that "some tens of thousands" of Soviet citizens are serving prison sentences for political or religious offences.[56] Anatoly Marchenko estimated on the basis of his experiences in Soviet penal institutions in the 1960s that there were "thousands" of such prisoners.[57] Edward Kuznetsov, a Leningrad Jew presently serving a sentence for his part in an attempt to hijack a Soviet aeroplane in 1970, has estimated that there are 2,000 political prisoners [58] Academician Andrei Sakharov estimated in late 1974 that the number of political prisoners was "between 2,000 and 10,000, not counting persons jailed for religious practices".[59]

P.I. Kudryavtsev, the same Soviet legal official mentioned above, has provided a significant clue for estimating the number of Soviet prisoners of conscience. Mr Kudryavtsev told Harold J. Berman that there were one million persons imprisoned in the USSR in 1957. Of these, he said, "about 1%" had been convicted of political crimes.[60] In other words, he acknowledged that there were then about 10,000 political prisoners in the USSR.

There is good reason to accept Mr Kudryavtsev's percentage estimate as an adequate minimum figure which still applies today. For one thing, Mr Kudryavtsev did not include in his figure persons convicted of religious offences, a category

56.　*New York Times Magazine,* 4 March 1973.
57.　Anatoly Marchenko, "Open Letter to the Chairman of the Soviet Red Cross and Others", 2 April 1968, reproduced in Anatoly Marchenko, *My Testimony* (Penguin Books, London, 1971), page 384.
58.　Edward Kuznetsov, *Prison Diaries* (Vallentine Mitchell, London, 1975), page 133.
59.　United Press International news agency dispatch, 30 October 1974.
60.　Harold J. Berman, "Soviet Law Reform — Dateline Moscow 1957", *Yale Law Journal,* Volume LXVI, Number 8, pages 1194-1196.

which was large in 1957 and remains large today partly as a consequence of the stringent regulations on religious practices implemented in the 1960s. Secondly, while many political prisoners have been released since 1957 on expiry of their sentences, many more persons have been imprisoned in connection with the development of more visible human rights activity in the 1960s and with the attendant introduction into the criminal codes of new political articles like 190-1 and 190-3 in the RSFSR Criminal Code. While a number of Soviet citizens and non-Soviet commentators have estimated that political prisoners number several times more than Mr Kudryavtsev's estimate of 1% of the total prison population, the latter's semi-official character makes it suitable as a minimum figure.

While there are no published official statistics on the size of the total Soviet prison population, it must be estimated to number at least one million Soviet citizens. That the Soviet prison population is very large was indicated by a recent authoritative official volume which noted that the labour output of prisoners has "a certain *[izvestny]* economic significance", and that production indicators for corrective labour institutions are established in the regular economic plans of the union republics.[61]

The United States Central Intelligence Agency recently calculated from satellite photographs that the Soviet prison population is slightly under 2.5 million.[62] Academician Andrei Sakharov has estimated a figure of 1.7 million,[63] while one Western authority has arrived at a minimum estimate of one million prisoners, a figure derived from the estimated total number of corrective labour institutions and the estimated population of each.[64]

Accepting as still applicable Mr Kudryavtsev's semi-official statement that 1% of Soviet prisoners in 1957 were political prisoners, and accepting as one million the approximate size of the present prison population, Amnesty International accepts that there are at least 10,000 political and religious prisoners in the USSR today.

61.    V.M. Blinov (editor), *Kommenatrii k Ispravitel'no Trudovomu Kodeksu RSFSR* (Moscow 1973) page 96. V.M. Blinov is the RSFSR Minister of Justice. Hereafter this title will be cited in English: *Commentary to the RSFSR Corrective Labour Code* (1973).
62.    *The New York Times,* 13 January 1974.
63.    Andrei Sakharov "Introduction" (December 1973) to Harrison E, Salisbury (editor), *Sakharov Speaks* (Collins/Fontana, London, 1975), page 43.
64.    Peter Reddaway, *The Forced Labour Camps in the USSR Today: An Un-recognized Example of Modern Inhumanity* (Brussels, 1973), pages 3-6.

# Maintenance of Prisoners

In contemporary Soviet penal law and theory, it is in the actual maintenance of prisoners (as opposed to their "reform" and "re-education") that the "infliction of suffering" is regarded as permissible and necessary.[1] In practice the degree of suffering inflicted upon Soviet prisoners is far greater than is ever admitted or condoned in official Soviet literature on the subject. This was implicitly acknowledged by a magistrate trying a political case in Armenia in 1969 when he said that "long-term imprisonment could have the most serious consequences for the health of the accused and for their further education".[2]

This report will deal with two aspects of the maintenance of prisoners in which is concentrated the greatest infliction of suffering upon them: the inadequate food norms and medical neglect.

## Food

Hunger as a permanent feature of colony and prison life is provided for in the corrective labour legislation. The determination of food rations for colonies and prisons and for different regimes is the responsibility of the USSR Council of Ministers. The currently operative diets for different categories of prisoners were laid down in 1972.[3]

Diet differs according to regime, although this is not provided for in law.[4] While prisoners under "ordinary" receive more and higher quality food than others, they are still on an inadequate diet. Most of the known prisoners of conscience are sentenced to strict or special regime. They thus receive especially low nutrition. Furthermore, it is prisoners of conscience who suffer most from the fact that prison administrations have considerable discretion in the provision of food. Prisoners can be put on reduced rations for "systematic and malicious" underfilfilment of their work norms.[5] The administrations' legal authority to

1. See above, and *Commentary to the Fundamentals of Corrective Labour Legislation of the USSR and Union Republics* (1972), page 33.
2. *A Chronicle of Current Events*, Number 16, page 13
3. *Commentary to the RSFSR Corrective Labour Code* (1973) page 146.
4. *Ispravitel 'no Trudovoye Pravo*, (1971), page 325.
5. *Commentary to the RSFSR Corrective Labour Code* (1973), page 146.

apply punishments for "violations of regulations" entails frequent deprivation of a prisoner's right to receive a food parcel or to spend small sums on purchase of supplementary food. Colony administrations regularly have prisoners placed in punishment cells (*PKT* or *SHIZO*) where, by law, food rations are further drastically reduced and warm food is provided only on alternate days.[6]

Raisa Palatnik, a Jewish librarian sentenced in 1971 to 2 years' imprisonment for "anti-Soviet slander", has described as follows the daily diet in an ordinary regime colony in Dnepropetrovsk region in the Ukraine:

> They fed us three times a day. In the morning, a thin soup of gruel, rotten fish and tea with three-quarters of an ounce [20 grams] of sugar. In the evening, the same, only without sugar. The main meal at lunchtime was cabbage soup made from water and bones. The second course at lunch was oatmeal or sometimes a small potato with vegetables. A little more than a pound of bread [500 grams] was distributed daily.[7]

Anatoly Marchenko has described the typical strict regime diet on the basis of his experiences of imprisonment in the 1960s:

Breakfast: 2 cupfuls of watery gruel
Lunch: 2 cupfuls of soup made with rotten cabbage and 2 ladles of thin gruel
Supper: 2 ladles of the same gruel, together with a piece of boiled cod the size of a matchbox.[8]

Ex-political prisoner Yury Gendler has described as follows the strict regime diet in Mordovian colony ZhKh 385/19 in 1973:

Breakfast: (served in half-hour shifts from 7.00 to 8.30 am) soup with potatoes and barley bread
Lunch: (served from 12.00 noon to 1.00 pm) cabbage soup, gruel with either pearl-barley, oatmeal, or millet; bread
Supper: (served from 5.00 to 7.00 pm in shifts) gruel; fish or fish-cakes; bread.[9]

A letter sent from colony ZhKh 385/19 in Mordovia in March 1974 and signed by six political prisoners gives a breakdown of the daily diet in a strict regime colony.[10]

6.  PKT is the standard acronym for *Pomeshcheniye Kemernogo Tipa:* "cell-type premises" SHIZO represents *Shtrafnoi Izolyator:* "punishment isolation block". Article 56 of the RSFSR Corrective Labour Code stipulates that prisoners placed in punishment cells or blocks shall receive food "at reduced rations".
7.  Quoted in *The New York Times,* 13 January 1974.
8.  Anatoly Marchenko, "Open Letter to Alexander Chakovsky, Editor of *Literaturnaya Gazeta* (27 March 1968), reproduced in Anatoly Marchenko, *My Testimony* (Penguin Books, London, 1971).
9.  Unpublished document by Yury Gendler, written after his emigration from the USSR in 1973.
10. Kronid Lyubarsky, *et al,* "Letter to the Moscow Human Rights Committee Regarding Camp Conditions" (March-April 1974).

| PRODUCT | I<br>CAMP<br>(strict regime) | II<br>PKT (PUNISHMENT BLOCK)<br>(special regime)<br>(Quantities in grams) | III<br>SHIZO CELL<br>(special regime) |
|---|---|---|---|
| Rye bread | 650 | 600 | 450 |
| Wheatmeal flour | 10 | 10 | 10 |
| Groats | 110 | 80 | 50 |
| Macaroni | 20 | 10 | - |
| Meat | 50 | 30 | - |
| Fish | 85 | 75 | 60 |
| Fat | 10 | - | - |
| Vegetable oil | 15 | 15 | 6 |
| Sugar | 20 | 10 | - |
| Potato | 450 | 350 | 250 |
| Vegetables (mainly cabbage) | 200 | 200 | 200 |
| Tomato paste | 5 | 5 | 5 |

According to international standards, the work done by prisoners in Soviet strict regime corrective labour colonies can be described as "very active".[11] The energy needed for a man working "very actively" for eight hours a day is 3,100-3,900 calories and for a woman 2,400-2,700 calories.[12] The above described strict regime diet (I) contains 2,600 calories. Thus, even on normal diet, prisoners on strict regime receive an insufficient calory ration. Prisoners on the PKT diet (II) receive 2,100 calories, even if they are required to do normal prisoners' work, while prisoners in SHIZO (III) are reduced to 1,300 calories.

According to international standards, the human organism requires a daily protein intake of one gram for each kilogram of body weight (provided the daily calory intake is sufficient, which is not the case in Soviet corrective labour colonies).[13] The above-described diets indicate that daily protein intake, too, is inadequate. One consequence is weight loss, since the daily protein intake cannot compensate for the loss of protein expended in energy. The net result is obvious. As the prisoner's physical condition deteriorates, his work capacity is diminished. For low work output he is liable to be punished with reduced diet. He is in a vicious circle resulting in chronic caloric and protein malnutrition.

This decline is exacerbated by deficiency of other essential nutrients (minerals and vitamins). The poor quality of nutrition in corrective labour colonies is one of the chief complaints constantly being made in appeals, protests and open letters to Soviet and international organizations (for example, The Red Cross) by prisoners.

11. *Energy and Protein Requirements* (World Health Organization Technical Report, Series Number 522, Geneva, 1973). See below, pages 72-78 for discussion of work requirements of Soviet prisoners.
12. Ibid.
13. *Nutrition and Working Energy* (FAO Freedom from Hunger Campaign, Basic Studies Number 5, Rome, 1972).

A 1973 report from a colony in Perm region reads:

We are served rotten potatoes and cabbage. Maggots and cockroaches are often found in the food, and the mess hall is frequently permeated by the stench of rotten fish. Despite chronic hunger, the inmates refuse their supper whenever rotten fish is served; this, however, does not improve conditions at all.[14]

A convict may see no fresh fruit or vegetables during the whole term of his confinement, and no milk unless he is put on an invalid hospital diet. There are reports of convicts eating quantities of wild flowers and grasses during summer months, perhaps to compensate for these deficiencies and/or to have something to chew and so lessen their hunger pangs.[15]

Inmates of Vladimir prison receive a lower food norm than prisoners in colonies. Prisoners who are transferred to Vladimir from elsewhere for some alleged misdemeanour are fed on reduced rations for the first month, and during that month they may not make use of the prison shop or of any food products brought with them. They are then placed on strict regime (the equivalent of a special camp regime, i.e., the most severe) for two months. Later they are shifted to the general prison diet and may use the shop to the extent of three roubles a month.

Many inmates and ex-inmates of Vladimir have criticized the especially low food norms in that prison. The following extract from an anonymous *samizdat* document (1973) provides the most detailed available description of the feeding of prisoners in Vladimir prison:

## Daily Norm of Nutrition: General Prison Norm

| | I<br>After July 1972 | II<br>Before July 1972 | III<br>Reduced Norm |
|---|---|---|---|
| | *(All Quantities in grams)* | | |
| Bread | 450 | 500 | 450 |
| Meat | 40 | 40 | - |
| Fish | 70 | 85 | 60 |
| Potatoes | 550 | 500 | 250 |
| Vegetables | 250 | 300 | 200 |
| Groats | 90 | 75 | 50 |
| Macaroni | 10 | 10 | - |
| Flour | 10 | 10 | - |
| Vegetable oil | 15 | 15 | 6 |
| Fat | 5 | - | - |
| Sugar | 20 | 15 | - |
| Salt | 10 | 10 | 10 |

14. "A Perm Camp" (1972-1973). Boris Shilkrot, a Jewish prisoner, went on hunger strike in Mordovian colony Zh Kh 385/17 in 1970 "because of the worms which one found in the soup everyday". "Bericht aus Valdimir", *Allgemeine Judische Wochenzeitung*, 30 August 1974.

15. See for example Anatoly Marchenko, *My Testimony*, page 214. A similar claim was made by Uwe Arp, a West German who served an 18-month sentence in a Mordovian colony from 1970-1972. See *The Daily Telegraph* (London), 10 April 1972.

58

Prisoners in a strict regime punishment cell or penal isolation block also get a reduced ration, but only every second day. On the other day they are issued with only 450 grams of bread, a tablespoon of salt and boiling water.

The diet under strict regime differs from the general diet in the amount of bread (400 grams) and of sugar. The other items are the same as in the general diet. The caloric value of the general prison diet is 2,000-2,100 calories; that of the reduced diet, 1,500 calories. The products from which the prisoners' food is made are of very low quality. There is only black bread — very damp and heavy.

## Weekly Menu for General Diet

(bread, sugar, sprats are issued in the morning for the whole day)

|  | Breakfast | Lunch | Dinner |
| --- | --- | --- | --- |
| Monday | Soup | I/ soup (different from breakfast II/ gruel | Potatoes |
| Tuesday | Gruel | I/ pea soup II/ gruel | Potatoes |
| Wednesday | Gruel | I/ borshch II/ gruel (often oatmeal | Gruel |
| Thursday | Gruel | I/ macaroni soup II/ gruel | Russian salad |
| Friday | Potatoes | I/ cabbage soup II/ gruel | Potatoes |
| Saturday | Gruel | I/ pea soup II/ gruel | Potatoes |
| Sunday | Gruel | I/ macaroni soup II/ gruel | Russian salad |

On the mornings of holidays (1, 2 May, etc) there is good herring instead of sprats, and vermicelli instead of gruel.

## Menu for Reduced Diet

| Breakfast | Sprats, bread, boiling water |
| --- | --- |
| Lunch | Soup or borshch (only one course) |
| Dinner | Gruel |

The soup is very watery, usually made of groats (wheat, barley, peal-barley, oats), macaroni or peas, with a negligible quantity of potatoes added. There is virtually no meat in the soup. The prisoners say: "They boil the meat in a bag and if a scrap leaks through somebody is lucky". Also, twice a week there is borsch or cabbage soup. Both are made from very sour cabbage that has not been washed. The same kind of cabbage is used in the Russian

salad. They also add sour pickles to the Russian salad. Sometimes instead
of the salad they give you a good boiled beet. The fish is sprats or pollack.
The sprats are salted or marinated, and fall apart at the first touch. The
potatoes are mashed — a kind of dark, watery puree. It is only in the
autumn that the potatoes are good. The gruel is made from the same
groats as the soup, but it is thicker (a bit) and without potatoes. Some
days prisoners with a bad stomach eat nothing for lunch, as a rule. For
example, on Wednesdays, when for lunch there is borshch made from
sauerkraut and oatmeal in which there are many oat husks.[16]

Prison diets I and II, the normal diets respectively after and before July
1972,[17] contain approximately 2,200 calories. This level of calory intake is
adequate only if the prisoner is sleeping eight hours, doing light activity work
four hours and is only sitting for the rest of the time (12 hours).

In practice this will never be the case. These diets are not sufficient for a
healthy man, let alone for a person who has been sent to Vladimir prison as a
punishment after spending months or years in a corrective labour colony on insufficient food rations.

Prison diet III[18] contains 1,500 calories and is sufficient only for a healthy
man resting 24 hours a day in bed with no physical activity whatever.

Still worse are the conditions in a strict regime punishment cell or penalty
isolation block. The prisoners there get diet III only every second day and the
other day only 450 grams of bread and water. This means approximately 1,200
calories and 42 grams of protein per day. This is in fact a starvation diet.

In the past, the harmfulness of the low prison food norms was partly
mitigated by the fact that inmates of prisons, being confined to their cells, were
not required to do heavy manual labour. However, some time in early 1975 it
became mandatory for inmates of prisons to do physical labour.[19] According
to a *samizdat* document written anonymously in March 1975 by an inmate of
Vladimir prison, prisoners receive an extra 100 grams of bread and some honey
each day if they work.

Nevertheless, the attitude of the prisoners themselves testifies to the meaning
of a stay in Vladimir prison. When Anatoly Marchenko returned from there to a
Mordovian colony in 1963, colony inmates immediately shared out with him
part of their own rations to help him recover from his ordeal and used "tricks"
to spare him from doing any work for the first few days.[20] Colony administrations today still rely on the threat of a stay in Vladimir prison as a basic means
of attempting to impose discipline among inmates of corrective labour colonies.
The threat is often carried out.

Diet in a colony or prison hospital brings some improvement, with an extra
ration of meat, fish and white bread, and a daily allowance of 200 grams of milk.

16. *A Chronicle of Human Rights in the USSR*, Number 7, pages 45-48. See also Boris
Shilkrot, "Bericht aus Vladimir", *Allgemeine Judische Wochenzeitung*, 30 August
1974.
17. See above, page 46.
18. See above, page 46.
19. Neither the corrective labour laws nor the commentaries thereon describe in any
detail the work conditions and norms of prison inmates. Likewise until recently
*samizdat* documents have not shed much light on work done by prison inmates.
20. Anatoly Marchenko, *My Testimony*, pages 197-208.

In practice, however, prisoners often experience some difficulty in obtaining proper medical attention and permission for transfer to a special diet. The most common medical complaint is stomach ulcer, and sufferers are by all accounts rarely given the diet they need. Many relapse into a chronic condition.

The prisoners pay for their food by way of an automatic deduction of about 42 kopecks (=24 pence sterling or 50 US cents) a day from their earnings. In winter this rises to 50 kopecks (29 pence sterling/61 US cents). According to Article 36 of the Fundamentals of Corrective Labour Legislation "convicted persons released from work on account of illness . . . shall receive food free of charge". Nevertheless prisoners have reported deductions of up to 75 kopecks daily (43 pence sterling/90 US cents) for a hospital diet.

In evaluating colony-prisoners' diet, it must be remembered that prisoners are required to do heavy physical work. In theory, only prisoners in special regime colonies are legally required to do "heavy physical work".[21] In practice, all prisoners are subject to exhausting labour conditions and high production norms.

In principle, the dependence of food rations on productivity is qualified by the oft-repeated statement that each prisoner enjoys a right not enjoyed by other Soviet citizens: the right to receive guaranteed nourishment whether he pays for it by work or not.[22] However, Article 36 of the Fundamentals of Corrective Labour Legislation reads, in part: "Food rations shall be differentiated depending on . . . the nature of the work done by convicted persons and their attitude to their work." The gradation of food rations for prisoners is theoretically justified by explicit reference[23] to the principle laid down in Article 12 of the Soviet Constitution: "He who does not work, neither shall he eat."

One form of making the amount of food received by prisoners dependent on their "attitude to work" consists of the system of supplementary purchases. Each penal institution has a "canteen" or "shop" where prisoners may purchase "food products and basic necessities". This right is preserved for prisoners "in the aim of interesting convicts in the results of their labour".[24] Therefore, they may spend on purchases of "food products and basic necessities" only such money as they have earned by their labour while in colony or prison, and the sum allowed for such purchases may theoretically be increased in the event of prisoners' overfulfilment of work norms.

The sum allowed for each prisoner for such purposes varies according to regime. Ordinary regime prisoners may spend 10 roubles (£5.80/US$12.20) per month, those on intensified regime seven roubles (£4.05/US$8.50). Strict regime prisoners are allowed five roubles' worth (£2.90/US$6.10). For special regime prisoners, and for those placed in punishment cells the allowance is reduced to two roubles (£1.15/US$2.40) each month.

An idea of the purchasing power of the allowance may be given by the 1974

21. RSFSR Corrective Labour Code, Article 37.
22. *Commentary to the Fundamentals of Corrective Labour Legislation of the USSR and Union Republics* (1972), pages 41-42.
23. Ibid, page 101.
24. Ibid, page 89.

retail prices of some basic food products:

> 500 gram tin of corned beed cost approximately one ruble 30 kopecks (75 pence sterling/US$1.58).
> 500 grams of the cheapest cheese cost 70 kopecks (40 pence/US 84 cents).
> 500 grams of a better quality cheese cost one rouble 75 kopecks. (£1.01/US$2.12).

The selection of permitted foodstuffs and other items available for purchase is limited, and their availability in any case sporadic. Some permitted foods are smoked herring, cheese, cheap sweets, margarine, jam, tinned vegetables and meat, and bread. The meagre shopping allowance has also to cover essentials such as soap, tooth powder, writing materials, etc. The two rubles allowed to special regime prisoners is *only* to be used for non-food items. Like the receipt of parcels and correspondence, use of the camp shop is in practice treated as a privilege rather than a right, and any small infringement of camp rules may mean deprivation of some or all of the shopping allowance for a month or longer. Another condition for using the shop is that only money earned by the prisoner may be used to purchase goods; money sent from relatives or friends is not spendable.

In camps in the far north or far east, shopping allowances are slightly higher to take into account the higher cost of food in these regions. However, even under optimum use of the shopping allowance (spending 10 roubles per month, buying the available food product with the highest energy contents and managing to consume this extra food at a regular rate over the whole month), the prisoner can obtain only an extra 250 calories per day, which still does not raise his diet to a level consonant with good health.

In fact the official *Commentary to the Fundamentals of Corrective Labour Legislation of the USSR and Union Republics* makes plain that the system of supplementary purchases is not intended to allow prisoners to escape from the hunger regime. This is the only possible explanation for the fact, stated expressly in the *Commentary to the Fundamentals of Corrective Labour Legislation of the USSR and Union Republics,* that only for convicts' purchase of food does the law set a spending limit, there being no such limit on spending in general. (Prisoners can spend unlimited amounts of money on state-published books, for example).[25]

The same policy of preserving the "hunger regime" is apparent in the list of types of punishment available to colony and prison administrations. They may order "deprivation of [a prisoner's] right to receive his next parcel or packet and the forbidding of him to purchase food products for up to one month".[26] In other words, this one punishment is intended to consist of cutting off both of the prisoner's sources of supplementary food. *The Commentary to the Fundamentals of Corrective Labour Legislation of the USSR and Union Republics* stipulates that this punishment is to include denial only of the prisoner's right to purchase food, and not of his right to purchase "basic necessities".[27]

25. Ibid, pages 91-92
26. RSFSR Corrective Labour Code, Article 53.
27. *Commentary to the Corrective Labour Legislation of the USSR and Union Republics* (1972), page 91

A legal — though very limited — way of supplementing one's diet is through food parcels. Depending on their regime of sentence, prisoners who have served one half of their sentence may each year receive as many as three parcels each weighing up to five kilograms. The range of permitted foodstuffs is very narrow: dry goods such as biscuits are allowed, but bouillon cubes are forbidden because of their meat content, and chocolate is banned because, in the words of one camp official, "it leads to excitement".[28] Visitors may bring certain very restricted items into the colony for their relatives. However, this small concession is tightly supervised. Like some other prisoners' rights, the receipt of these parcels is in practice treated as a privilege, and the right to receive them is often cancelled as a punishment.

In an effort to make prisoners totally dependent on their institutional rations, a decree was issued by the RSFSR Supreme Soviet on 7 June 1972, virtually prohibiting the import of food. The decree reads in part:

> For the illegal transmission, concealment from examination or attempted transmission by whatever means, to convicted persons, of articles, food products, money, liquor, and also other substances prohibited from use in corrective labour institutions, it has been laid down that where such activities do not involve criminal responsibility the guilty parties shall be subject to an administratively imposed fine of from 10 to 50 roubles, or to measures of social pressure."[29]

In 1972, Academicians Sakharov and Leontovich protested publicly at the imminent ratification of this decree and sent a telegram to the Chairman of the RSFSR Supreme Soviet expressing their disagreement with it, and maintaining that:

> The culpability for illegal transmission of food products to prisoners which is established by the decree is an official indication of the existence of a regime of chronic starvation in our camps and prisons. No one would resort to illegal transmission if there were no necessity for it. The decree opens up possibilities of making the tragic situation of prisoners ... even worse, by instituting searches of prisoners and their visitors. We call upon deputies of the Supreme Soviet to speak out for a reform of corrective labour legislation, with the aim of putting an end to the intolerable torturing of prisoners through starvation."[30]

So far as is known, this protest was ignored and the decree was ratified, and still stands.

It is noticeable that Soviet prisoners are almost always employed on industrial work of some sort or on timber-cutting, but almost never on agricultural work, in spite of the annual shortage of farm labour in many areas during the sowing and harvest seasons. This phenomenon received partial explanation in 1968 in an officially-published monograph on penal theory. The authors recommended strongly against putting prisoners to work on farms, partly because:

28. Anonymous *samizdat* "Letters from Potma" (January 1972), published in English in *Human Rights in the USSR* (Brussels), September 1972.
29. *Vedomosti Verkhovnogo Soveta RSFSR*, 15 June 1972.
30. *A Chronicle of Current Events*, Number 26, pages 263-264

it is impossible to limit prisoners' consumption of many food items which are produced in such colonies (milk, eggs, vegetables, fruit, etc). Thus the food rationing levels which exist for prisoners and also the regulations on parcels and hand-delivered packets lose their significance.[31]

Thus, not only the law itself but governmental decrees and the policy of colony and prison administrations ensure that prisoners remain hungry as a basic condition of their imprisonment. Though not acknowledged formally, the punitive intention of this policy has been affirmed orally many times by officials. For example when the Ukrainian prisoner Valentyn Moroz complained to the deputy procurator of the Mordovian camp administration that prisoners seriously ill with stomach ulcers were being kept on a starvation diet, the official replied: "That's just what the punishment consists of — hitting the stomach."[32]

Anatoly Marchenko has summarized the results of this policy:

> Thus the camp administration wields a powerful means of exerting physical pressure on political prisoners — a whole system of escalation of hunger. The application of this system results in emaciation and avitaminosis [a disease caused by lack of vitamins]. Some prisoners are driven by the permanent malnutrition to kill and eat crows and, if they are lucky, dogs. In the autumn of 1967 one prisoner from camp 11 in Mordovia found a way of getting potatoes while in the hospital section. He over-ate and died — the potatoes were raw.[33]

## Medical Care

Obviously such lengthy deprivation can, and in many cases does, have serious consequences for prisoners' health. The combination of low-grade, badly cooked, hastily eaten food with heavy labour in unhealthy conditions and a harsh climate causes some prisoners to emerge as chronic invalids. Most inmates suffer from stomach ulcers and other gastric complaints after two or three years. Colony and prison medical facilities are inadequate to cope with the health problems of prisoners subjected for long periods to these detrimental conditions.

By law each colony must have a first aid post or larger medical unit (*medpunkt* or *sanchast* in Russian), including a doctor's surgery, a dispensary and a laboratory. One colony in each district may have a full-scale hospital: in the Mordovian complex for example, this is attached to colony 3 at Barashevo.

According to the *Commentary to the Fundamentals of Corrective Labour Legislation of the USSR and Union Republics,* "all the achievements of medical science" are utilized in corrective labour institutions.[34] Yet standards of medical care have been a very common cause for complaint by prisoners. The staffing of medical facilities in the colony and prison system is deficient. This is to some degree understandable. There are many colonies and prisons with medical posts

31. I.V. Shmarov, F.T. Kuznetsov and P.E. Podymov, *Effektivnost' deyatel 'nosti Ispravitel 'no-Trudovikh Uchrezhdenii* (Moscow, 1968), page 158. See also Peter Reddaway (editor), *Uncensored Russia* (Jonathan Cape, London, 1972), page 203.
32. Valentyn Moroz, "A Report from the Beria Reservation", in *Boomerang: The Works of Valentyn Moroz* (Smoloskyp Publishers, Baltimore, 1974), pages 49-50.
33. Anatoly Marchenko, "Open Letter to the Chairman of the Soviet Red Cross and others" (2 April 1968), in Anatoly Marchenko, *My Testimony,* page 38.
34. *Commentary to the Fundamentals of Corrective Labour Legislation of the USSR and Union Republics* (1972), page 141.

to be filled and skilled, experienced medical personnel very likely prefer work among the civil population to service in places of imprisonment. Medical work in corrective labour institutions is made particularly unappealing for doctors by the fact that colony and prison doctors must work under administrations whose demands frequently conflict with and over-ride medical judgements. Colony doctors are assigned officers' rank in the MVD and wear MVD insignia.

A frequent complaint by prisoners is that the medical units and even hospitals are staffed by newly qualified, inexperienced doctors who are assisted by junior medical officers known in the Soviet Union as *feldshers* — semi-skilled practitioners with no graduate qualifications. Sometimes *feldshers* are recruited from among prisoners themselves and hastily trained in the essentials of first aid and minor surgery. A typical medical unit would include: two doctors, a dentist, one or two *feldshers,* two nurses and two orderlies. There might be a small ward with in-patient facilities for treatment of minor illnesses. More serious complaints would be treated by specialists who visit each colony at intervals of two to three months, and for whom there is always a long waiting list.

At Mordovian colony ZhKh 385/19 in January 1972, the 120-bed medical unit had three therapeutists, one surgeon and one dental technician, all with comparatively little experience. Hours of work were from 10 am to 5 pm. In the evenings, during the night, and on holidays and at weekends no doctor was on duty and no medical service at all was available: the entire unit was manned for emergencies by one *feldsher,* who was an ex-tractor driver.[35]

To the lack of trained staff in many colonies and prisons is added the shortage of proper medical equipment and materials. A 1973 *samizdat* report from a colony in Perm region (in the Urals) states:

> Medical care is on a low level. A majority of the inmates are serving
> sentences ranging from 15 to 25 years; many suffer from ulcers,
> tuberculosis and heart conditions. The only hospital is 60 kilometers
> away by truck over unimaginably bad roads. The camp dispensary lacks
> the barest necessities or medication. When prisoner Melikian suffered an
> ulcer attack and prisoner Fyodorov a paralyzing stroke, they had to be
> carried from the construction site on boards for lack of a stretcher. No
> medication was available and no medical aid was given to either one.
> (Fyodorov urgently needed a neuro-pathologist and Melikian was in need
> of immediate surgery). They were not even taken to the hospital. But
> even had they been taken there, they would not have received help,
> because the hospital is not staffed with specialists. Many sick prisoners
> who are in a serious condition do not want to go to the hospital
> because it is nothing more than a prison where the wards are simply
> locked cells, the windows have solid blinds, sanitary requirements are
> disregarded, and patients suffering from contagious diseases are not
> segregated from the others. There are no toilets, merely a latrine
> bucket. The journey is so exhausting that sick prisoners have apprehensions about ever reaching the hospital alive.[36]

35. "Letters from Potma" (1972).
36. "A Perm Camp" (1972-1973).

Prisoners have frequently complained that what medications are available in colonies are often misused and that drugs are administered long after their recommended period of usefulness has expired.[37]

An example of incompetence in the use of medications is provided by the case of Mikhail Bartashuk, a Baptist prisoner in Brest region in Byelorussiya. When Mr Bartashuk entered the colony in 1970 he was officially qualified as a "work invalid". At the time he was in good health except for a chronic disability (the exact nature of which has not been learned by Amnesty International). His health deteriorated in colony conditions, and he applied to the doctor for treatment for high blood pressure and heart problems. He was treated in late 1973 with tablets and injections which brought about partial paralysis and almost complete blindness. His wife was later told by doctors that he would not regain his eye-sight in his left eye.[38]

Edward Kuznetsov (a Leningrad Jew sentenced to 15 years' strict regime for participation in an abortive hijacking attempt in 1970) developed distressing stomach ulcer symptoms in Mordovian colony ZhKh 385/1 in 1971. Captain Tabakov, head of the medical unit, at first refused to believe that Mr Kuznetsov was ill. He finally prescribed entereseptol, a medication used in treating dysentry.[39] Mr Kuznetsov then undertook a hunger strike, and after one week was admitted to the colony's hospital. Here the doctor diagnosed gastritis and prescribed some tablets to conteract nausea. After one week in hospital, Mr Kuznetsov was returned to the colony, his condition untreated.[40]

Amnesty International and other international human rights organizations regularly receive requests from prisoners' relatives in the USSR asking that politically neutral doctors be sent to examine inmates of Soviet prisons and colonies. Numerous requests are received for sending drugs and medications to prisoners particularly in need of them.

There has never been a case where a non-Soviet doctor was allowed to examine or treat a Soviet prisoner. Presumably this is explained by the official view that Soviet doctors are in no need of professional help from abroad. Less explicable is the invariable refusal to allow medications to be sent to prisoners. Until 1966 it was possible for prisoners' families to send them vitamins and drugs authorized by a colony doctor. These were subject to "censorship" on arrival to prevent the smuggling of narcotics, and many drugs prescribed in good faith and sent by relatives never reached the patient. In 1966 the import of drugs and any other medicaments was banned outright: any which arrived thereafter were held back by the censor regardless of appeals by colony medical officers.

Staff shortages and lack of adequate facilities contribute to the poor medical treatment universally reported by prisoners. However, an important factor is the official attitude to prisoners' medical needs. This attitude is often one of indifference and, at colony level, of overt hostility. According to Article 37 of the

37. See for example the account of former political prisoner Hilel Sbur, "In Potma", *Possev* (Frankfurt am Main), April 1973.
38. Undated letter from the prisoner's wife to the Soviet leaders and to the Baptist "Council of Prisoners' Relatives".
39. Edward Kuznetsov, *Prison Diaries* (Vallentine Mitchel, London, 1975) pages 207-208. See also the anonymous "Letters from Potma" (January 1972). in *Human Rights in the USSR* (Brussels), September 1972.
40. "Letters from Potma" (1972).

Fundamentals of Corrective Labour Legislation:

> The procedure for rendering medical aid to persons deprived of liberty, the use of public health medical institutions and agencies and the enlistment for this purpose of medical personnel shall be determined by the Ministry of the Interior of the USSR and the Ministry of Public Health of the USSR.

In practice this gives decision-making authority on medical matters to the Ministry of the Interior and the corrective labour administrations.

The day-to-day operation of camp medical services is subject not only to difficulties inherent in colony life but to the administrations' attitudes toward prisoners' requests for medical treatment.

The procedure for seeing the doctor is complicated: long queues, a bureaucratic registration system, hasty and often unsympathetic treatment. There are many malingerers hopefully seeking authorized respite from work, and these swell the queues to the detriment of genuine patients. A sick prisoner who joins the queue early in the morning is unlikely to see the doctor before the time when he is due to begin his day's work. If he then fails to obtain a medical certificate exempting him, or if he is seen by a *feldsher* who is not authorized to issue a certificate, he may be regarded as absent without leave and, however ill, will suffer the consequences.

There are reports of doctors treating genuinely ill prisoners as wholesale malingerers. A Jewish prisoner in a Mordovian colony who went to a doctor because of heart trouble was told to "spend less time learning Hebrew".[41] Lieutenant Colonel T.P. Kuznetsov, head of a medical commission in Perm colony VS 389, told prisoners that his job was not to treat them but to force them to work. Among the would-be patients whom Lieutenant Colonel Kuznetsov classified as "fit for work" were two amputees.[42]

Colony doctors' recommendations are subject to administrative approval. An application by a doctor for a certain drug to be supplied, or his recommendation that a prisoner be transferred to lighter work or moved to a warmer climate for medical reasons, may be over-ruled by administrative personnel.

Amnesty International recently learned for example, that in October 1974 doctors in a camp in Kherson region (in the Ukraine) urgently recommended that the Jewish prisoner Alexander Feldman be moved to a civil hospital for treatment of a severe liver condition. This recommendation was over-ruled by the colony administration on grounds that Mr Feldman's condition was not suffuciently dangerous to justify such transfer.

There is no doubt that colony medical personnel are in a very difficult position vis-à-vis the authorities, and that most of them do the best they can in the circumstances. However, a number of instances of deliberate neglect on the part of colony doctors have been reported. In May 1974, during the long hunger strike by political prisoners in Perm colony VS 389/35, non-striking prisoners demanded that those on hunger strike be force-fed to prevent their deaths. Major Yarunin, the doctor in colony VS 389/35, replied: "Forced feeding will be resumed on the basis of medical symptoms, as soon as they begin to smell of

41.   "Letters from Potma" (1972).
42.   *A Chronicle of Current Events,* Number 30, page 97.

Sketch made of Yury
Galanskov in a
Mordovian corrective
labour colony, probably
in 1969.

acetone."[43] (The body gives off a smell of acetone when in an acute stage of starvation).

Similar reports have emerged from Vladimir prison. In 1974, Boris Shilkrot wrote with reference to his stay in Vladimir between March 1971 and August 1972:

> In order to get a doctor to come in an emergency one had to pound on the door for hours. I recall the case of a Latvian who developed a blocked intestine. He rolled about in his sleeping place for four days before they put him in the prison hospital.[44]

There have been a number of cases where prisoners have died as a direct consequence of medical neglect. For example in 1969 Rashid Dinmukhamedov, aged 49, slit his veins shortly after arriving in colony 10 in Mordovia. He received no medical attention for over five hours: the duty officer said the hour was too late to summon a doctor. Mr Dinmukhamedov died from loss of blood.[45] In the summer of 1973 Lieutenant Colonel Kuznetsov of Perm colony VS 389 classified the prisoner Kurkis as "fit for work", although Mr Kurkis had not worked for many years because of an ulcer condition. After his first day of work, Mr Kurkis suffered an ulcer attack, and Lieutenant Colonel Kuznetsov refused to come to treat him because of the "bad weather". Mr Kurkis died.[46]

43.  "The Journal of a Month-Long Hunger Strike", *A Chronicle of Human Rights in the USSR*, Number 10, page 30.
44.  Boris Shilkrot, "Bericht aus Vladimir", *Allgemeine Judische Wochenzeitung*, 30 August, 1974.
45.  *A Chronicle of Current Events*, Number 17, page 72.
46.  Ibid, Number 20 page 97.

The most famous and well documented of the numerous known cases of death through medical neglect was that of the poet Yury Galanskov.[47] Mr Galanskov was sentenced in 1968 to 7 years in a corrective labour colony for his active defence of the writers Sinyavsky and Daniel. While serving his sentence in colony ZhKh 385/17 in Potma (in Mordovia), he developed a duodenal ulcer. The administration refused to allow him to receive the special food (honey, for example) sent by relatives. Besides being kept on a diet which was detrimental to him in his condition, he was compelled to continue working an eight-hour day. Colony officials answered the complaints of Mr Galanskov's mother with the assertion that Mr Galanskov was not ill but was just "a hooligan who shirked his work".

According to Alexander Ginzburg, a friend of Mr Galanskov who served his sentence in the same colony, there was only one doctor in the colony. Mr Galanskov received almost no medical treatment in 1972. He refused to submit to a surgical operation because he believed the colony doctor to be incompetent. He appealed to international organizations for medical assistance,[48] saying he had lost hope of receiving medical treatment in the colony. On 18 October, after his ulcer had burst, Mr Galanskov was operated upon. The operation was carried out not by the colony doctor, but by a fellow prisoner who had medical training but no surgical experience. After the operation the administration refused to allow even this person to visit Mr Galanskov or to transfer Mr Galanskov to a civil hospital. When a qualified doctor was finally summoned from Moscow (450 kilometers to the northwest), it was too late. Mr Galanskov had died on 4 November 1972 at the age of 33.

Soviet law provides a device for early release of prisoners who are seriously ill. Article 100 of the RSFSR Corrective Labour Code states:

> Convicted persons who are suffering from chronic mental illness or other serious illness preventing the further serving of their sentence can be freed by a court from further serving their sentence. The procedure for freeing such persons from further serving their sentence is defined by legislation of the USSR and RSFSR.
>
> An application for release from further serving of sentence shall be brought to the court by the head of the organ charged with execution of the punishment. Together with this application there shall be sent to the court the conclusion of a medical commission and the personal file of the convicted person.

By requiring examination of the prisoner's "personal file", this article leaves room for consideration of subjective factors such as the prisoner's "behaviour" or "attitude to work" in the decision whether to release seriously ill prisoners. Nevertheless, Article 100 as a whole gives prominence to the objective state of the prisoner's health and would seem to offer a real possibility for more humane treatment of ill prisoners.

However, despite the large number of prisoners eligible for early release under

47. See ibid, Number 28 pages 9-11, for documentation of the circumstances of Mr Galanskov's death.
48. The text of his appeal was published in *Le Point* (Paris), 12 February 1973.

Article 100, this article is largely ignored in practice. No prisoner adopted by Amnesty International has ever been released on medical grounds. We have heard of no other cases of release of prisoners of conscience under the terms of Article 100.[49]

Apparently, however, it is this article which has been invoked in the numerous transfers of troublesome political prisoners to psychiatric hospitals on the grounds of their alleged "mental illness".[50]

One such prisoner is Yury Belov, who was sentenced in 1967 to 5 years' imprisonment for having written a *samizdat* essay "Report from the Darkness".[51] In 1970 he was transferred from a colony to Vladimir prison, apparently as a disciplinary measure. In the autumn of 1971, new criminal proceedings were initiated against him for "anti-Soviet agitation" allegedly carried out within the prison. However, in December 1971 he was sent to the Serbsky Institute of Forensic Psychiatry in Moscow for a psychiatric examination. He was diagnosed as "mentally ill" and in May 1972 transported from Vladimir to the special psychiatric hospital in Sychyovka (in Smolensk region). According to *A Chronicle of Current Events*, the head doctor of this institution told Belov "that they would treat him until he changes his opinions".[52]

Another prisoner to whose disadvantage Article 100 has been applied is Algirdas Zypre.[53] Mr Zypre, a Lithuanian, joined a group of Lithuanian partisans in 1944 while German and Soviet troops fought for possession of the Baltic republic. At the time he was 14 years of age, and he was moved to join the partisans both by nationalist sentiment and by the fact that his mother had been sent to a Siberian prison colony in 1944 on account of her ownership of a farm.

In 1958, Mr Zypre's former partisan activities were discovered and he was sentenced to 25 years' imprisonment. Shortly thereafter new criminal legislation came into force setting the maximum term of imprisonment at 15 years.[54] In 1973, having served 15 years' imprisonment, Mr Zypre began petitioning legal authorities for his release. His petitions were rejected in the summer of 1973. When he persisted in his efforts to obtain release, he was taken in September 1973 from Perm colony VS 389/36 to Moscow's Serbsky Institute for psychiatric diagnosis. (According to an anonymous *samizdat* document, Mr Zypre was first diagnosed by local psychiatrists employed in the corrective labour system). In 1974 Mr Zypre was transferred from Moscow to a hospital psychiatric ward in Mordovian corrective labour colony ZhKh 385/3. His family believes that he is being treated with drugs.

49. Cf. *Khronika Tekushchikh Sobitii*, Number 33, page 31.
50. The formal procedures for psychiatric examination of convicted persons is described in Ya.M. Kalashnik, "Psychiatric Expert Examination of Convicts, Witnesses and Victims", in G.V. Morozov and Ya.M. Kalashnik (editors), *Forensic Psychiatry* (International Arts & Sciences Press, Inc., White Plains, New York, 1970). This volume is a translation of *Sudebnaya Psikhiatriya* (Moscow, 1967).
51. Mr Belov's case is described in *A Chronicle of Current Events*, Numbers 9, 10 26 and 27.
52. Ibid, Number 26, page 34.
53. Amnesty International's information on Mr Zypre comes from letters from members of his family living outside the USSR and from an anonymous *samizdat* document (late 1971) describing conditions in the psychiatric department of the hospital service in the Mordovian corrective labour complex.
54. RSFSR Criminal Code, Article 24.

The nature and quality of medical facilities provided for Soviet prisoners deviates sharply from legal stipulations that prisoners are to receive all necessary medical treatment. Even more does it conflict with claims that Soviet penal policy reduces to a minimum the infliction of suffering on prisoners. This is incurred in part by ommission — the shortage of trained personnel and facilities — and in part by commission — the reluctance to give serious consideration to the real medical needs of many prisoners. Medical neglect dovetails with chronic hunger and with overwork to give to Soviet penal institutions a more punitive character than is justified by any standards, let alone by the high standards proclaimed by Soviet authorities.

# Reform of Prisoners

Soviet corrective labour law and all officially-approved literature on the subject assert that the Soviet penal system is infused with the principle that imprisonment has as its goal the reform of the prisoner. This principle is humanitarian in conception. Paradoxically, however, it contains considerable danger for prisoners if it is not carefully defined and applied scrupulously in accordance with regulations.

As has been shown above, contemporary Soviet corrective labour law has opted for the view that the reform of prisoners aims not merely at preventing recidivism (repeated commission of crimes by the prisoner) but at changing the prisoner's consciousness: his moral outlook, his relation to his fellow men and to labour.[1] In theory, establishing such a high goal requires that each prisoner be exhaustively studied by prison authorities so that an "individual program" for his rehabilitation can be worked out.[2] In practice, the injunction to examine each prisoner minutely gives prison authorities wide authority to find faults in prisoner's behaviour and impose punishments or further restrictions on them. The recent *Commentary to the RSFSR Corrective Labour Code* lists "the application of measures of encouragement and of punishment" as one of the administrations' functions in carrying out individual education with prisoners. Amnesty International has never heard of a case of a "measure of encouragement" being applied to the benefit of a prisoner of conscience.

This "individual program" is not to be accepted by the prisoner on a voluntary basis, out of his own recognition that he is in need of thorough-going reform. The prisoners' "correction and re-education" is compulsory, and he must accept the "program" devised for him by the camp or prison administration.

Obviously the risk of arbitrariness in this sphere is great. Even the most humane prison administration is liable to err in evaluating prisoners' needs in the way of reform and in devising the "program" for fulfilling those needs. The danger of arbitrary decisions in this matter is especially great because, as is officially stated, it is not desirable that camp and prison administrations should be fettered in this complex task by abstract rules and regulations. Therefore

1. See above, pages 40-42.
2. *Commentary to the Fundamentals of Corrective Labour Legislation of the USSR and Union Republics* (1972), page 113.

these administrations are allowed a great deal of leeway in deciding how to "correct and re-educate" prisoners under their control.

As is apparent from much of what has been written above in this report, the MVD administrations of Soviet corrective labour institutions are not characterized by the high principle, judgement and self-discipline necessary to achieve the humanitarian goals laid down by Soviet penal law and theory. A study of material available on Soviet prison conditions leaves the net impression that the goal of rehabilitating prisoners is not taken seriously either by administrators or prisoners. The goal of rehabilitation of prisoners is totally outweighed in the administration of colonies and prisons by considerations of security and by the "punitive" element. Political prisoners especially are informally given to understand that this is the case. For example, in Mordovian special regime colony ZhKh 385/1, KGB Captain Kochetkov told Edward Kuznetsov in 1971:

> You're on special here. This is not a corrective but a punitive institution. Our job is to bend you, until you're like putty in our hands. Do you understand?[3]

So divorced is the theory from reality that in none of the *samizdat* documents emanating from Soviet camps and prisons do prisoners even call for adherence to the theory that prisoners should be "rehabilitated". Prisoners appear to regard the theory as "utopian" and in referring to it confine themselves to abuses committed by administrators in the guise of "correction and re-education" of prisoners.

According to Article 7 of the Fundamentals of Corrective Labour Legislation of the USSR and Union Republics, there are four basic means for the "correction and re-education" of prisoners:
- "the regime of serving sentence"
- "socially useful work"
- "political and educational work"
- "vocational instruction"

The first of these means of "reforming prisoners" is based on the principle that "punishment" in itself serves to re-educate prisoners by exercising a deterrent effect on them. This process has been discussed above in its most important aspect, the hunger regime. The latter three means of reform are supposed in theory to be devoid of any infliction of suffering on prisoners.[4]

## Work

According to law, "every convicted person shall have the duty to work".[5] The place assigned to prisoners' labour in Soviet corrective labour law and theory is explained in part by the high esteem given to labour in general by Marxist-Leninist doctrine:

> Labour is a universal means of education for people. On the basis of participation in socially useful labour is formulated the psychology of a toiler, the feeling of comradeship and collectivism. In labour are

3.   Edward Kuznetsov, *Prison Diaries,* page 181.
4.   Natashev and Struchkov, *Osnovy Teorii Ispravitel 'no-Trudovogo Prava,* pages 87-88.
5.   *Fundamentals of Corrective Labour Legislation of the USSR and Union Republics,* Article 27.

moulded the socially useful qualities of a man. Also by means of socially useful labour is gained reform of convicted persons.[6]

To this end the RSFSR Corrective Labour Code stipulates:

The production and economic activity of corrective labour institutions must be subordinated to their basic task — the correction and re-education of convicted persons.[7]

However, the obligation of prisoners to work is explained by another principle as well: "He who does not work, neither shall he eat."[8] It is intended that, as much as possible, prisoners shall pay by their own productivity for the costs of their prison maintenance.[9] This principle applies as well to all categories of invalids and to persons over the legal age of retirement.[10]

The RSFSR Corrective Labour Code (Articles 37-42) lays down in broad terms the conditions under which prisoners are to work. However, the most recent *Commentary to the Fundamentals of Corrective Labour Legislation of the USSR and Union Republics* acknowledges that these regulations are only general in character.[11] Specific details of prisoners' labour are laid down by the administration of each corrective labour institution.

In practice, the prisoners' work in no way leads to the enhancement of their consciousness or to their "reform", as called for by corrective labour theory. Prisoners' work is a form of punishment, a fact acknowledged by the Soviet newspaper *Kazakhstanskaya Pravda* (14 March 1973) in a rare public reference to convict labour:

The work carried out by prisoners is basically hard labour, and output norms are maximal. But there is nothing to be done about this. A labour colony is not a rest home. It is a place for serving out punishment. Here it is necessary to work. By the sweat of one's brow.

Prisoners perform a wide variety of duties both inside and outside the colony. Forced labour is used on a fairly large scale on construction sites in remote areas of the country to which it is difficult and costly to attract a sufficient quantity of free workers. Work of all types is compulsory: non-working prisoners receive a reduced food ration and no payment. The type of work to which a convict is assigned usually depends not upon any professional skills he may possess but upon the facilities available and the regime specified in his sentence. Generally speaking, the stricter the regime, the heavier, more unpleasant and more dangerous the work performed.

A prisoner serving under **ordinary regime** is normally likely to do indoor piece-work (sewing, for example) or not too strenuous workshop jobs (such as carpentry and metalwork). Kitchen staff, some orderlies, storekeepers and book-keepers are usually recruited from among criminal prisoners serving under

6.  *Commentary to the Fundamentals of Corrective Labour Legislation of the USSR and Union Republics* (1972), page 34.
7.  *RSFSR Corrective Labour Code*, Article 37.
8.  Natashev and Struchkov, op.cit. page 125; *Commentary to the Fundamentals of Corrective Labour Legislation of the USSR and Union Republics* (1972), page 101.
9.  *Commentary to the Fundamentals of Corrective Labour Legislation of the USSR and Union Republics* (1972), page 101.
10. *Commentary to the RSFSR Corrective Labour Code* (1973), page 92.
11. *Commentary to the Fundamentals of Corrective Labour Legislation of the USSR and Union Republics* (1972), page 35.

ordinary regime for less serious offences. Prisoners are permitted to move freely about the colony zone in the course of their duties.

Prisoners under **intensified regime** often work in a larger workshop or factory, perhaps making furniture, polishing radio and television sets, assembling electrical appliances, printing envelopes or making cardboard boxes.

The prisoner on **strict regime** (the majority of known political prisoners are in this category) must do heavy manual labour such as laying sewers, road-building, lumber work or work in factories where air pollution is dangerous to health and conditions are noisy and a nervous and physical strain.

**Special regime** (also common for prisoners of conscience) entails manual labour, usually of an extremely strenuous nature: stone-quarrying, reclaiming marshland, digging sand, logging, brick-making, and large-scale construction — chemical plants, for example. Work is done under strict guard, and prisoners may be transported to and from the site by armed guards accompanied by dogs, often over a distance of 40-50 kilometers each day.

According to Article 37 of the RSFSR Corrective Labour Code, prisoners are to be assigned work "with consideration of their work-capacity". A recent *Commentary* elaborates:

> Consideration of the convict's work-capacity is obligatory for the administration . . . An insufficient workload, and, even more so, over-taxing work correspond neither to the educative nor the economic goals of labour nor to considerations of health. Putting convicts to over-taxing labour would contradict the law's position that the execution of punishment does not have as a goal the infliction of physical suffering.[12]

However, the work capacity of prisoners is largely neglected in assigning labour and production norms to prisoners. It is frequently reported that even invalids and cripples or seriously-ill persons are assigned to arduous physical labour. The following statement appeared in a *samizdat* appeal to the International Red Cross by a group of political prisoners in a Mordovian colony in 1971:

> For example, of 480 prisoners in camp 3/1, 134 are invalids of the second group, while 108 are invalids of the third group. These are mainly the very old, finishing 25-year sentences, who miraculously survived the hells of Vorkuta, Magadan and Norilsk. Most of them participated in national movements and had the audacity to resist the national policy of the party, applied with cruelty in many areas. Goaded by the fear of every possible stricture, hardship and final starvation, they are driven to the workshops "to exploit their residual labour capacity", according to a cynical expression of an officer at Dubrovlag, Captain Suchkov.
>
> Their old played-out bodies cannot sustain the high rates of production; it happens that men fall dead at their work. Only the completely crippled are left to themselves — men who can scarcely move about on crutches.[13]

---

12. *Commentary to the Fundamentals of Corrective Labour Legislation of the USSR and Union Republics* (1972), page 102.
13. *Samizdat* "Appeal by Nine Political Prisoners to the International Red Cross" (December 1971).

By law, prisoners on all regimes must work no more than an eight-hour day.[14] Generally this norm is respected, although some ex-prisoners have reported that the work is sometimes extended to 9, 10 or even 12 hours for three or four days a week according to the colony's production schedule. Normal shift-hours are 8 am to 4.30 pm (first shift) and 4 pm to 12.30 am (second shift) with a half-hour meal break for lunch or supper respectively. Sunday or one other day a week is free. In some places only alternative Sundays are free.[15]

Large construction projects generally have an overall time schedule. In the case of most other types of convict labour, there is usually an individual norm to be fulfilled. Norms are high and prisoners may be assigned work with which they are unfamiliar and be expected to fulfil the norm nevertheless.

Prisoners report that norms are continually being increased and payment rates for piece-work lowered. A prisoner who spent some time in three Mordovian colonies in the 1960s reported that over a period of one and a half years the norm for polishing television sets rose from four to 14 per eight-hour shift.[16] Elsewhere, 52 radios were expected to be polished and 65 pairs of mittens sewn in a similar shift.[17] On the other hand Yury Gendler has reported that his norm of milling 360 wooden watch-cases, although initially exhausting, soon became a habit and with practice he was able easily to produce the requisite amount in four hours (half a shift) and thus earn himself considerable extra money.[18]

Colony ethics, however, particularly among criminal prisoners, frowned upon overfulfilment of more than 5%, even when this was easily possible, in spite of the productivity rewards — extra portions of soup, increased shopping allowances and parcels etc. Raisa Palatnik (a Jewish librarian who spent two years in a colony in Dnepropetrovsk region in the Ukraine after being convicted of "anti-Soviet slander" in 1971) has stated that in her ordinary regime colony, payment of one ruble 50 kopecks (87 pence sterling/US$1.83) was payable for each 10% achieved over and above the monthly norm.[19]

Consistently good work and exemplary conduct may count towards early release, but this is only rarely applied to political prisoners. On the other hand, failure to report for work, whatever the reason, may be punished by cancellation of privileges. Repeated failure to work or to achieve the norm may mean incarceration in an isolation cell for a period of days, weeks or months. Convicts have been known to stage go-slows with production down to 10-40%, and even strikes, in protest against rising norms, unfair transfers of workers, etc. There is little evidence that these have ever had the intended effect, and participants usually find themselves in the punishment block. Illness is treated unsympathetically by team leaders anxious to fulfil norms.

According to law, safety provision for work in corrective labour institutions

14. RSFSR Corrective Labour Code, Article 38.
15. See for example, "A Perm Camp" (1972-1973).
16. Confidential document written by a former prisoner of conscience after his emigration from the USSR.
17. Confidential document written by a former prisoner of conscience after his emigration from the USSR.
18. Unpublished document written by Yury Gendler after his emigration from the USSR in 1973.
19. Unpublished document written by Raisa Palatnik after her emigration from the USSR in 1973.

76

must meet the standards stipulated by labour legislation for all Soviet enterprises.[20] In practice, however, prisoners' work conditions are usually unpleasant and often dangerous.

Yury Gendler has reported that in his Mordovian colony the noise level in the woodworking shop was so high that prisoners stuffed cotton wadding into their ears and wore their winter hats with the earflaps down even in summer. Ventilation was so bad that sawdust hung in the air and covered everything.[21]

Prisoners in a Perm colony reported similar lack of safety precautions in 1972. The air in plastics-working shops was filled with harmful white magnesium oxide "sand", which extended even to the prisoners' barracks. There was no ventilation in the shops.[22]

Raisa Palatnik worked in a sewing-room with 200 women prisoners. The work involved sewing gloves, overalls, underwear, jackets and quilt covers. In 1968, the norm for jackets had been 100; in 1972 it was 145 — using the same 10-year-old equipment. There was no ventilation, first aid equipment or disinfectant. If an accident occurred, the victim had to walk back to the living zone for treatment.[23]

Industrial injuries are common. For example, Father Pavel Adelheim, a priest arrested in June 1970 and sentenced to 3 years' hard labour, had to have a leg amputated as a result of a work injury sustained in a colony.[24]

Representative of prisoners' accounts of colony labour conditions is the following extract from a letter sent out by a group of prisoners in Mordovian colony 19 in 1972:

> [In the machine-tool] shop the most dangerous part of the process is the removal of the finished piece and the installation of a new one. There is no provision for switching off the press during this technical operation, which is a serious infringement of technical safety completely inadmissable in an outside environment. The rotating reamer may easily injure the prisoner's hand: such injuries are fairly common. In addition, sharp, hot chips fly out from under the reamer. To work in gloves is forbidden in case the glove — and with it one's hand — becomes caught and pulled into the reamer. As well, there are splashes of emulsion which burn the skin, fumes, and horrible noise, not only from one's own press but also from the entire workshop. Shimon Levit has small cuts all over his hands . . . No one is able to fulfil the work quotas, which are tremendously high; failure to fulfil means punishment . . . The loading work is even worse. We all fear assignment to this particular job, which consists basically of loading and unloading railway wagons. The work is very difficult and dangerous, and one may be awakened [for work] at any time of the day or night without advance warning. Even on Sundays, one works.
>
> . . . At first glance, sewing mittens in the camp workshop appears to be fairly light work. Such shops exist in almost all the camps. Women

20.   RSFSR Corrective Labour Code, Article 38.
21.   Unpublished document written after Mr Gendler emigrated from the USSR in 1973.
22.   "A Perm Camp" (1972-1973).
23.   Unpublished document written by Raisa Palatnik after her emigration from the USSR in 1973.
24.   A Chronicle of Human Rights in the USSR, Number 2, page 17.

confined for political reasons are engaged exclusively on this work, but
even they find the job tiring. What can one say about those who have
to do it? . . . Excessively high demands must be met in dimly lit buildings
using machinery which is continually breaking down . . . Sylva Zalmanson
suffers from constant backache and dizzy spells due to the continuous eye
strain. Because of acute eye strain Yury Fyodorov [another political
prisoner] has been transferred from sewing mittens to turning them inside
out — work which is less conducive to strain and acute conjunctivitis. He
is lucky, because the sewing norm can be fulfilled by few. Even healthy
persons are unable to achieve it, and all suffer the consequences.

 . . . In outside construction work the situation is aggravated by the
fact that it is almost impossible to endure the Mordovian frosts in the
so-called "special work clothing" . . . Changes and transfers are frequently
made; at any time one may expect a transfer to even more difficult and
strenuous work. This happened to [two political prisoners] Altman and
Shepshelovich, who are now both working on a concrete mixer in pene-
trating winds . . .[25]

According to law, prisoners are to be paid for their labour at the rates established for all Soviet workers.[26] However, most of their earnings disappear into
automatic deductions for their upkeep. The prisoner is guaranteed receipt of only
10% of his earnings.[27] Most of this sum goes automatically into the prisoner's
account, where it is kept to cover any future fine, penalty for damage and such-
like.

Prisoners are not allowed to be in possession of cash. However, as was described above, they are allowed to spend in coupons a set amount from their
earnings on "food and basic necessities" and on books retailed by the government. Officially, this is said to be "in the aim of interesting convicts in the results
of their labour".[28]

Because of the insignificant size of real pay and the lack of opportunity to
spend more than tiny sums of money, prisoners' only real work incentive is the
possibility that the availability of food might be changed to their benefit or
disadvantage depending on the administration's evaluation of their work performance.

Prisoners who overfulfil their norms are allowed to spend from two to four rubles
extra each month (depending on work conditions) on "food and basic necessities".[29] This extra food-purchasing privilege can mean a significant increase
in the rate of nourishment of a prisoner. However, former prisoners have remarked on prisoners' difficulty in deciding whether the extra food purchased
compensates for the additional expenditure of energy and physical strength
necessary to obtain high norms. The granting of this privilege is at the discretion of camp authorities, and it is normally awarded only for exceptional
labour output.

25.  "Letters from Potma" (1972).
26.  RSFSR Corrective Labour Code, Article 39.
27.  RSFSR Corrective Labour Code, Article 39.
28.  Commentary to the Fundamentals of Corrective Labour Legislation of the USSR
     and Union Republics (1972), page 89.
29.  RSFSR Corrective Labour Code, Article 24.

In the case of political prisoners, the right to food purchases more often figures in the range of "disincentives" available to the camp administration. Political prisoners are often accused of having a "bad attitude" to their labour, a catch-all charge which embraces any disfavour they may incur with the camp authorities. On the basis of this charge, which may or may not have anything to do with the prisoner's actual productivity, political prisoners are often deprived of the right to spend even the established minimum amount from their earnings on food. Furthermore, prisoners who are charged with "systematic and malicious" failure to meet production norms are liable to have even their regular rations reduced.

## *Political Education*

The official aim of "political education" work with prisoners is to educate them "in the spirit of honest attitude to labour, of exact fulfilment of the laws and respect to the rules of socialist communal life, of a protective attitude to socialist property . . ."[30]

A variety of political-educational measures are called for by law, including "agitation and propaganda work" and "explanation of Soviet legislation".[31]

Guided by these general norms, the administration of each corrective labour institution "can apply any means and methods of pedagogical influence, provided these do not contradict the rules of regime established in the legal norms".[32] Greatest emphasis is placed upon the political education classes which are held at least once weekly (except in prisons, whose inmates are not allowed to leave their cells except for their work duties and for their exercise period). These classes last up to two hours, and during them members of the colony administration discuss current affairs and political news and other officially approved topics such as the history of the Communist Party. By all accounts these lectures and the discussions they provoke are conducted on a very low level and are universally resented. Political prisoners, many of whom are highly educated, find these political classes particularly degrading.

In an essay written in a Mordovian colony in 1966, the Ukrainian historian Valentyn Moroz wrote:

> At the "political training" sessions conducted by semi-literate corporals for artists and writers, the prisoners once began a discussion with Senior Lieutenant Lyubayev (camp number 11) using the [UN] Declaration of Human Rights as an argument. He retorted indulgently: "Listen, but that is for Negroes."[33]

Edward Kuznetsov, serving a 15 year sentence in a special regime corrective labour colony for his part in an abortive hijack attempt in 1970, wrote in 1971 in his *Prison Diaries*:

> The last class I went to, Lieutenant Bezzubov gave us the priceless information that, "in China the Zionists and the Red Guards are on the

30.   RSFSR Corrective Labour Code, Article 43.
31.   Ibid, Article 44.
32.   *Commentary to the Fundamentals of Corrective Labour Legislation of the USSR and Union Republics* (1972), page 35.
33.   Valentyn Moroz, "A Report from the Beria Reserve", in *Boomerang: The Works of Valentyn Moroz*, page 55.

rampage. But the Chinese people are not stupid — they'll show them!"
The academic level of these lectures is truly breath-taking!"[34]

Nonetheless, the attitudes which prisoners show toward and in these classes can be used by the administration "in ascertaining the extent of their correction and reform".[35] Prisoners of conscience seem always to resist the pressure to conform to the official viewpoint in these classes. A minimum consequence of their continued "dissidence" is that political prisoners are thus disqualified from being considered for early release.

The corrective labour law does not make attendance at these classes compulsory, and the *Commentary to the Fundamentals of Corrective Labour Legislation of the USSR and the Union Republics* states that it is impermissible to treat attendance at them as an obligation of prisoners.[36]

However, a 1972 MVD directive (number 020) circumvents this legal norm and makes it punishable for prisoners not to attend political classes. To avoid formally contradicting the legal norm that attendance at political classes must be voluntary, the directive categorizes political classes as part of the colony "order of the day" and makes non-attendance punishable as violation of the "order of the day".[37]

In practice, colony and prison administrations do not generally strive for the "political re-education" of prisoners of conscience. Such prisoners almost always have deep political or religious convictions which have been formed in the face of the highly-organized agitation and propaganda campaign aimed at all Soviet citizens and for which they were willing to risk imprisonment. Any serious attempt to alter the convictions of such persons would require far more intellectually sophisticated "teachers" than are available in corrective labour institutions, where political classes are conducted by low-ranking MVD personnel. In his 1973 monograph on penal theory, the leading Soviet jurist, M.D. Shargorodsky, wrote:

> Illegality and inhumanity destroy the educational significance of a punishment, and there remains of it only suffering, only chastisement [kara].[38]

Yet statements by Soviet prisoners leave no doubt that "illegality" and the infliction of suffering are in their experience the dominant characteristics of life in Soviet colonies and prisons. The convictions of political and religious prisoners regularly serve as grounds for punishment. Any effort by a prisoner to communicate his politically dissident views to others is liable to bring transfer to a more severe regime. A number of prisoners of conscience have been tried in prison for such activity and received additional sentences.

34.   Edward Kuznetsov, *Prison Diaries* (Vallentine, Mitchell, London, 1975) page 216. These diaries were smuggled out of Mordovian colony ZhKh 385/1 some time in 1971. Two men, Victor Khaustov and Gabriel Superfin, were sentenced to imprisonment in 1974 on charges of having helped smuggle the *Prison Diaries.*
35.   RSFSR Corrective Labour Code, Article 43.
36.   *Commentary to the Fundamentals of Corrective Labour Legislation of the USSR and Union Republics* (1972), page 78.
37.   See for example the *samizdat* "Letter to the Moscow Human Rights Committee Regarding Camp Conditions" (1974), signed by six political prisoners (Kronid Lyubarsky et al) in Mordovian colony ZhKh 385/19.
38.   Shargorodsky, op.cit. pages 22-23.

*Samizdat* documents emerging from Soviet corrective labour institutions regularly include accounts of incidents in which camp and prison authorities make crude and ignorant remarks in response to the political and legal claims raised by prisoners or in response to religious prisoners' request for respect of their right to worship.

The attitude of colony officials to religious prisoners was described in 1973 by a group of former Soviet prisoners advocating better treatment for political prisoners in all countries of Europe:

> The hunt after religious literature is accompanied in prisons and camps by ferocious persecution of religious believers. The dispersal of prayer meetings in the camp areas, punishment by solitary confinement for failure to report for work on major religious holidays (such as Easter and Christmas), the forbidding of any kinds of rites, even preaching and giving the sacrament for dying prisoners — these are the methods of "educational" influence with the help of which they try to eradicate religious dissent.[39]

Jewish prisoners are frequently singled out for special abuse. The following statement by a group of prisoners in Perm colony VS 389/35 is representative of many prisoners' criticisms on this subject:

> The camp authorities inculcate nationalistic conflicts and agitate other inmates against Jews. KGB Captains Maruzan and Ivkin stress in their conversation with non-Jewish inmates that all nationalities of the USSR must take a stand against Jews, particularly in labour camps. The administration provokes anti-Jewish incidents, utilizes informers and spies, and uses false witnesses in order to be able to impose additional punishment upon the Jews. Inmates who have had contact with Jews are summoned for discussions during which anti-semitic sentiments are expressed, and they are told that protests against arbitrariness in camp rules are only profitable to the Zionists . . . The Jews are forbidden from practising their religious traditions . . . and forbidden to congregate even for a few minutes; such gatherings are immediately regarded as a Jewish assembly, a synagogue. Conversation in Hebrew or Yiddish is subject to punishment because these languages are not understood by the guards and therefore their content cannot be checked. The study of Hebrew is prohibited. Internal letters in Hebrew or Yiddish are banned and confiscated.[40]

The open contempt with which the convictions of prisoners of conscience are treated is not conducive to their re-education in the spirit desired by the law. On the contrary, political prisoners' experiences in corrective labour institutions usually strengthen their dissident convictions by providing what they regard as corroboration of their criticisms of institutionalized illegality and arbitrariness in their country.

39. *Samizdat* "Appeal to the European Security Conference" by nine former political prisoners. Undated, but apparently written in August 1973. Partial text in English in *A Chronicle of Human Rights in the USSR*, Number 7, pages 48-49.
40. "A Perm Camp" (1972-1973).

## *Vocational Instruction*

The fourth prescribed means for "correction and re-education" of prisoners is "general education and professional-technical study".[41] By law, corrective labour institutions are required to provide general education up to the eighth grade for all prisoners who do not have such education. The law further allows for high school education for prisoners where facilities are available.[42] No information is available on the manner of application of these legal norms covering general education.

It is clear, however, that prisoners who have high professional qualifications do not benefit from any "professional-technical study" while in prison. In this respect the present corrective labour legislation is not as "progressive" as the 1933 legislation, which stated that "the organization of labour of those deprived of freedom must facilitate retention and raising of their qualifications and the gaining of new qualifications".[43]

In educational facilities as in labour requirements contemporary Soviet corrective labour institutions do not meet this requirement with regard to professionally trained persons. Those who suffer most from this are prisoners of the "intelligentsia" category, the category to which most political prisoners (but not most religious prisoners) belong. Prisoners have reported that they are subject to "starvation of the intellect". Prisoners cannot read up-to-date books or articles in the fields of their specialized qualifications. A letter from political prisoners in Mordovia in the spring of 1974 stated: "Emerging from camp after many years of imprisonment, a man finds himself fully unqualified as a specialist."[44]

This situation belies official statements that the Soviet corrective labour system aims to make it possible for prisoners to take up a normal life in society. With regard to political prisoners, it is counter-productive of this goal. On emerging from a colony or prison, such persons find themselves incapable of returning to their former profession, not only because of general discrimination against persons with records of political dissidence, but because they have lost their technical or academic expertise. In the case of prisoners who have committed common law crimes, this situation is hardly conducive to prevention of recidivism. In the case of prisoners convicted for manifestations of political dissent, exclusion from their professional careers is liable only to encourage further manifestation of dissent.

In sum, the Soviet corrective labour system does not fulfil the rehabilitative and educative task assigned to it by corrective labour legislation and theory.

41.   RSFSR Corrective Labour Code, Articles 47-50.
42.   Ibid, Article 47.
43.   RSFSR Corrective Labour Code (1933), Article 70.
44.   Kronid Lyubarsky *et al*, "Letter to the Moscow Human Rights Committee Regarding Camp Conditions" (1974). See also "An Open Letter from the Astronomer Lyubarsky to the Executive Bureau of the World Federation of Scientists, London, and the Executive Committee of the Congress for Cultural Freedom, Paris" (October 1974) in *A Chronicle of Human Rights in the USSR* (New York), Numbers 11-12.

# Relationships between Prisoners and Administrators

In any prison system the relationship between prison administration and prisoner is characterized by an element of coercion. Within the walls of any prison anywhere there exists the danger that prison authorities will abuse their right to use coercion by arbitrarily subjecting prisoners to brutal or degrading decisions.

Recognizing this danger, Soviet jurists have demanded the fullest possible regulation of the day-to-day relations between prison authorities and prisoners. However, as has already been indicated in this report, great discretion is left to the administration of each corrective labour institution. This is officially regarded as necessary because of the need for flexibility in administrative reaction to the wide variety of problems which require decision in the operation of a penal institution.

In theory and according to the written law, the possibility of administration abusing their discretionary authority is minimized by the powerful supervisory rights of the procuracy and of public supervisory commissions. In practice, the only check on the behaviour of colony and prison authorities is the Ministry of Internal Affairs (MVD), in whose jurisdiction the corrective labour system is placed. However, the MVD itself has a long record of hostility to the interests of prisoners and especially to political prisoners.

The authoritative *Commentary to the RSFSR Corrective Labour Code* (edited by the RSFSR Minister of Justice, V.M. Blinov) warns against any effort by local or administrative officials to assume the legislative organs' authority to make law.

> Only the legislative organs can introduce a new norm or change or replace an existing law if they find this necessary. As long as a law is not replaced according to the established order it must be observed exactly . . . The law excludes any actions whatever which, under the pretext of their expedience go beyond the limits of the law and do not conform to it.[1]

However, prison authorities are guided in the routine administration of their institutions less by the general rules set down in the corrective labour code than by a host of administrative "instructions" issued by the MVD, the texts of which are mostly kept secret even from the prisoners. Emanating from the ministry which commands the corrective labour system, and being more detailed than

1.   *Commentary to the RSFSR Corrective Labour Code* (1973), page 25.

the legislative norms, these instructions have greater operative authority for prison officials than do the provisions of the corrective labour codes. It was the plethora of such instructions which supplanted the 1933 RSFSR Corrective Labour Code and rendered it inoperative by 1953, a development which Soviet jurists have since condemned.[2]

Even when these instructions contradict the letter or spirit of provisions of the corrective labour law they are given precedence. One example of such circumvention of the law was cited above: the making of non-attendance at political classes a punishable offence.

The instruction most often cited by prisoners in this respect is MVD Instruction Number 020 of 14 January 1972. This decree required a large number of changes in treatment of prisoners. Each of the changes brought in by Instruction 020 further restricted prisoners' rights and enhanced the opportunity of prison authorities to harass and punish prisoners.[3] For example, Instruction 020 lifted the RSFSR Corrective Labour Code's 15-day limit on confinement to SHIZO (punishment isolation cell) and made the duration of such punishment subject only to evaluation of the prisoner's health. The instruction sharply restricted the variety of food products available for prisoners' purchase, and extended the grounds for confiscation of prisoners' correspondence.

Instruction 020 is only one of many administrative instructions which regulate concrete conditions in Soviet corrective labour institutions. According to many reports from prisoners, the strong tendency of current instructions is toward increasing hardships for prisoners. This represents an erosion of the authority which was originally ascribed to the Soviet corrective labour codes in an effort to prevent a recurrence of the anarchy which characterized the Soviet prison system under Stalin.

## Prison Security

Soviet law names as the first requirement of corrective labour institutions the maintenance of security.[4] The application of this obligation is such that prisoners serve their sentences in a condition of abject subjugation to the prison authorities. They are given to understand clearly that their well-being is at the disposal of the latter.

At any time prisoners can legally be subjected to a body search or to search of their possessions. The list of personal possessions allowed to prisoners is set by administrative regulation and is quite meagre. Prisoners are not allowed to have money or valuables in their possession. Possession of radio or television sets is always prohibited. Prisoners may possess books, although Instruction 020 has restricted the number of allowed books to five. Bibles and religious literature are banned, as are playing cards or any form of gambling game. Prisoners are not allowed to possess artists' materials such as paints, coloured crayons and brushes.

2.   *Commentary to the Fundamentals of Corrective Labour Legislation of the USSR and Union Republics* (1972), page 5.
3.   The provisions of Instruction Number 020 are most fully listed in *A Chronicle of Current Events*, Number 33, pages 9-10. See also Lyubarsky *et al*, "Letter to the Moscow Human Rights Committee Regarding Camp Conditions" (1974).
4.   Fundamentals of Corrective Labour Legislation of the USSR and Union Republics, Article 19.

*Above:* Corrective labour colony ZhKh 385/11 in the Mordovian ASSR, apparently taken in the late 1960s.

The rigidity with which colony and prison administrations enforce the restrictions on personal possessions varies from institution to institution and from time to time. However, the unlimited right of search is regularly used to provide a pretext for punishing individual prisoners and as a means of harassing prisoners of conscience. It was reported from a Perm colony in 1973 that the colony's deputy commandant, Major Fyodorov, "when spotting an extra book among someone's possessions, would throw it to the floor and trample it under his boots".[5]

Certain other routine regulations seem to contradict the legal requirement that punishment does not aim at "degrading human dignity".[6] The following regulation established in all corrective labour institutions after the issuing of Instruction 020 conflicts with reasonable standards of civility:

> When meeting a member of the camp personnel or other persons visiting the camp in an official capacity the convict must greet them by standing up and, in the warm seasons of the year, taking off his cap. The convict must use the polite form of address to the camp personnel and call them "citizen" or "citiziness", followed by their rank and official position.[7]

Instruction 020 also restored the former practice whereby prisoners are required to wear a patch bearing their family name and their prison serial number on their clothing. Particularly disturbing are recent reports (emanating from colonies both in Mordovia and in Perm) that prisoners are as a matter of routine shorn bald.[8]

The rules of discipline impinge directly on prisoners' correspondence rights.

5. "A Perm Camp" (1972-1973).
6. Fundamentals of Corrective Labour Legislation of the USSR and Union Republics, Article 1.
7. Lyubarsky *et al,* "Letter to the Moscow Human Rights Committee Regarding Camp Conditions" (March-April 1974).
8. See "Anonymous Report to World Society on the Strengthening of Stalinist Tendencies in the USSR and Especially in Camps for Political Prisoners" (1974), and Lyubarsky *et al,* "Letter to the Moscow Human Rights Committee Regarding Camp Conditions" (1974).

According to law, prisoners may receive an unlimited number of letters. The number of letters prisoners may send out of the camp is restricted to three a month (intensified regime), two a month (strict regime) or one a month (special regime). There are no restrictions in ordinary regime camps. For prisoners confined to punishment cells, the allowance may be reduced to one letter in two months. Instances have been reported of prisoners being completely deprived of correspondence rights for as long as a year.

Both incoming and outgoing mail is censored and may be confiscated, sometimes without notification, either as a form of punishment or on the grounds of objectionable content. This applies particularly to mail to and from families and friends of political prisoners and mail from abroad to Jewish prisoners. Some prisoners — and their families — go for months without receiving a letter. All references to prison or colony life are struck out of letters sent by prisoners.

Another ground for censorship and delay is the language in which a letter is written: letters in any language other than Russian (for example, Ukrainian, Georgian, Kazakh, etc) may first be sent to the capital of the appropriate republic (Kiev, Tbilisi, Alma-Ata, etc) where they are officially translated and returned to the colony censor, a process which may take up to three months. For political prisoners from non-Russian republics (many of whom are serving sentences for alleged nationalism and use their own language or dialect on principle — which is not an infringement of any law), this is a particularly cruel and humiliating form of censorship. Mail to prisoners from abroad rarely reaches its destination.

Prisoners' legal right to receive parcels is also violated in the name of security. Prisoners in colonies may receive parcels only after having served one half of their sentence, no matter how long the sentence. The number of parcels which a prisoner is entitled to receive depends upon his regime. Ordinary regime prisoners may receive three parcels each year; intensified regime prisoners may receive two parcels each year; prisoners on strict or special regime may receive one parcel each year. Parcels, whether mailed or delivered by hand, may not exceed five kilograms in weight. As well as such parcels, all prisoners are entitled each year to two smaller packages weighing one kilogram and containing paper and linen products and dry confections (excluding chocolate). In the past they could, in addition, subscribe to journals and newspapers and receive parcels of books ordered through a special postal book service. Only Soviet publications could be ordered; foreign books were prohibited. However, in November 1972 this right was rescinded, reportedly by oral instructions to book dealers.[9]

Because of prisoners' chronic hunger, food parcels are especially important to them. Since the adoption of the present corrective labour legislation, more restrictions have been placed on the number of food items which can be sent in parcels to prisoners. Persons who send parcels containing prohibited items (such as chocolate or meat products) are liable to a fine of up to 50 roubles (£29/US $61).[10]

However, prisoners are not in practice guaranteed the benefit of even parcels

9.  *A Chronicle of Current Events,* Number 28, page 43.
10. RSFSR Supreme Soviet Decree (7 June 1972), published in *Vedomosti Verkhovnogo Soveta RSFSR,* 15 June 1972.

86

whose contents conform to regulations. Many parcels addressed to prisoners "disappear" in the same way as do letters to them. According to the *Commentary to the Fundamentals of Corrective Labour Legislation of the USSR and Union Republics*, colony and prison authorities are obliged to search each incoming parcel, but must do so in the presence of the prisoner to whom the parcel is addressed. Amnesty International's attention has been drawn to a number of cases in which those conducting such searches have deliberately ruined the contents by opening and mixing together all food items in the parcels. This practice is not routine, but it is exemplary of the widespread abuse of security measures as a means of causing unjustified discomfort to prisoners and degrading their dignity.

The law requires that prisoners (except those on strict regime) be allowed a certain number of visits each year. Two types of visit are allowed. Ordinary (short) visits, lasting up to four hours and taking place in a visiting hall, and private (long) visits, lasting up to three days. Private visits are officially regarded as valuable in maintaining family ties, and they are normally granted only to spouses. They are meant to be conducted in a room fitted with all that is necessary for conjugal life.

Under ordinary regime prisoners are allowed four ordinary and two private visits annually; under intensified regime three ordinary and two private visits (during which they must continue to work); under strict regime, two ordinary visits and one private visit; and under special regime, one ordinary and one private visit. However, each visit is subject to approval by the colony or prison administration.[11] Even apart from the regular practice of deprivation of prisoners' right to their next visit, colony and prison administrations frequently use the exigencies of discipline and security as a pretext for disrupting visits.

Ordinary visits are supervised. Physical contact between the prisoner and his visitor is prohibited. Conversation between prisoners and their visitors in colonies located in the RSFSR must in practice be in Russian to ensure the supervising personnel that unapproved of information is not passed either into or out of the institution.

Relatives of political prisoners are sometimes singled out for humiliating treatment by the camp authorities. Since the 1972 decree of the RSFSR Supreme Soviet prohibiting the import of certain (most) items into prisons and camps, visitors to Mordovian and Perm camps have been subjected to an undignified compulsory body search on arrival.

In Perm colony VS 389/35, the Ukrainian writer Ivan Svitlichny wrote in a complaint to the procuracy in August 1974:

> When my wife came to visit me in September 1973 they did not simply search her, but stripped her naked, forced her to squat, etc. That is, they subjected her to a procedure which was extremely degrading to her human dignity. V.V. Sarnachnaya, the wife of prisoner Z. Antonyuk, was subjected to the same operation.[12]

The visit is cancelled if visitors refuse to consent to this process. They are

11. *Commentary to the Fundamentals of Corrective Labour Legislation of the USSR and Union Republics* (1972), page 77.
12. *Khronika Tekushchikh Sobitii*, Number 33, page 28.

searched again on departure to prevent the transmission of letters, *samizdat*, etc, out of the colonies. This humiliating procedure is nowhere sanctioned by law.

## Discipline and Punishments

It is in the context of this routine disrespect for prisoners' persons that the administrations' right ro impose punishments must be understood. Some of the most common pretexts for application of punishments are:
- lodging complaints which are regarded as dangerous
- absence from work for whatever reason
- failure to fulfil norms
- refusal to doff cap to prison or camp officer
- injury or self-mutilation for whatever reason
- singing, knocking messages on cell wall, making noise
- possessing "unauthorized" items
- lateness for roll-call, meal, work
- hunger striking
- wearing unauthorized clothing for work
- refusal to attend political classes
- playing cards
- making political remarks
- signing protests and appeals to Western organizations

Colony and prison administrations show great flexibility in deciding what constitutes grounds for punishment. Such actions as wearing carpet slippers, rising from bed "three minutes late" and brewing tea concentrate have served as pretexts for formal punishment.

Article 34 of the Fundamentals of Corrective Labour Legislation gives a comprehensive list of officially approved penalties:
- warning or reprimand
- extra duty for cleaning the premises and the territory of the place of confinement
- deprivation of one visit to the cinema or a concert, and of participation in athletic games
- deprivation of an ordinary visit
- deprivation of the right to receive a regular parcel delivered by mail or in person, and of the right to buy foodstuffs for up to one month.
- cancellation of the improved conditions envisaged in Articles 23, 24 and 25 of the present Fundamentals
- placing up to 15 days in a punishment cell (PKT) of convicted persons in prisons without permission to attend work or study
- placing up to 15 days in a penal isolation block (SHIZO) with or without permission to attend work or study
- placing up to 6 months in cell-type premises of persons in ordinary, intensified or strict regime corrective labour colonies; up to one year in isolation cells in colonies with a special regime; and, in prisons, transfer to a strict regime for the period prescribed in Article 15 [2 to 6 months]; transfer of persons from the ordinary living quarters of a special regime colony into cell-type premises in the same colony.

The less severe of these punishments are regularly used to deprive prisoners of visits and vital parcels. However, even the most severe punishments are used frequently and on petty grounds.

Prisoners sent to punitive detention in corrective labour colonies are normally subjected to special regime conditions in so-called "cell-type premises" (PKT is the Russian abbreviation) or isolation cells (*Shtrafnoi Izolyator,* or SHIZO for short). Inmates of prisons may be placed in a *kartser* (solitary confinement cell) for up to 15 days. There exist special statutes regulating the physical character of punishment cells and blocks.

> . . . it is categorically forbidden to create punishment and disciplinary isolation units of such a fashion that spending time in them harms the health of convicted persons.[13]

However, conditions in punishment cells (both PKT and SHIZO) often are such as to harm the health of prisoners. Some SHIZO cells are said to be damp and either too well ventilated or not at all: occasionally they are underground. In winter, water may freeze in the cells; in summer they can be stifling. The prisoners sleep on bare boards and sanitary facilities are primitive. The cells do not usually have wash-basins (occasionally there is a metal basin or bowl for general purpose use). Prisoners are obliged to use a part of their already restricted exercise period in order to wash. SHIZO cells have a latrine bucket which the prisoner himself empties daily. After doing this he has nowhere to wash his hands. Exercise time is reduced. Food rations are reduced and prisoners receive warm food only on alternate days.

The imposition of deprivations and discomfort on prisoners in punishment cells can be found in most prison systems. In Soviet colonies and prisons, the administration of such punishments is often marked by brutality. The spirit in which punishments are applied is illustrated by the way in which the administration of Perm colony 36 treated a group of prisoners who in 1972 staged a hunger strike in protest against Instruction 020:

> During the first four hours of the hunger strike they were threatened and insulted. Later the administration resorted to more drastic measures. No medical aid was given to the strikers although such aid is stipulated in the rules regarding hunger strikes. They were then summoned one by one to the guardhouse, where the entire camp administration was present together with KGB staff. When they refused to obey Instruction Number 020 and terminate their hunger strike, the emaciated inmates were punished with cell confinement of between 5 and 15 days, after first being wrestled to the ground, handcuffed and shaved.[14]

Furthermore, insufficient attention is given to the state of health of prisoners subjected to long periods in punishment cells. In May 1974, prisoners in Perm colony VS 389/35 were told by medical and other officials of the region's Administration of Corrective Labour Institutions that Soviet law does not prohibit putting invalids into punishment cells and that there is no legal requirement that a prisoner be medically examined before being put in a punishment cell.[15]

13.  *Commentary to the Fundamentals of Corrective Labour Legislation of the USSR and Union Republics,* (1972) page 131.
14.  "A Perm Camp" (1972-1973).
15.  "The Journal of a Month-Long Hunger Strike" (1974).

The poor medical conditions of many prisoners makes the application of such punishments dangerous. Yet prisoners with conditions such as stomach ulcers are regularly subjected to the harsh conditions of PKTs and SHIZOs. A group of Soviet Jewish citizens, writing to United States senators in early 1974 about the maltreatment of Alexander Feldman (a Jewish would-be emigrant imprisoned on apparently fabricated charges of "hooliganism"), said that "people who have seen such punishment tell that young men are carried out after 15 days — unable to walk".[16] Mr Feldman had been subjected to six weeks in a punishment cell despite a severe kidney ailment, and the same Jewish citizens cited the report of his fellow prisoners that "his skin is turning yellow and he cannot stand up".[17] Such reports are common.

Confinement to a punishment cell (whether PKT, SHIZO or *kartser*) represents a temporary change in the regime on which a prisoner is kept. However, "bad behaviour" may also be punished by a formal, long-term change in a prisoner's regime.

Short of the death penalty (see below), the most severe form of punishment available to a colony administration is to transfer a prisoner to Vladimir prison. Located in the ancient Russian city of the same name, Vladimir prison is the most severe penal institution in the USSR (excluding the special psychiatric hospitals).

Vladimir prison is reserved for persons guilty of "grave crimes", "especially dangerous recidivists", and persons transferred from corrective labour colonies by way of punishment. Numerous political prisoners are transferred there from other penal institutions.

Among the many Amnesty International adoptees who were so transferred in 1973 and 1974 were Sergei Malchevsky, Yakov Suslensky, Aleksander Sergiyenko, Kronid Lyubarsky and the Marxist dissidents Yuri Vudka and Yuri Fedorov. In July 1974, Vladimir Bukovsky, who in 1973 had completed his 2-year sentence in Vladimir prison, was transferred there for 3 years after participating in a hunger strike in a corrective labour camp in Perm region.[18] The astronomer Kronid Lyubarsky, who in the spring of 1974 headed the list of prisoners signing a letter to the Moscow Human Rights Committee describing violations of legality in the Mordovian colonies, was ordered to be sent to Vladimir prison in October 1974. Colony officials charged that Mr Lyubarsky "had not gone on the path of correction", while a local procurator charged that he "had not changed his views".[19] When Mr Lyubarsky arrived at Vladimir prison he was immediately placed on strict regime. According to *A Chronicle of Current Events*, Mr Lyubarsky was also subjected for two months to an extra-legal feeding norm known as the "punishment cell ration".[20]

Despite the severe conditions in Vladimir prison, seriously ill prisoners are often transferred there. For example, Kronid Lyubarsky has had most of his

16.   Quoted in *Jews in the USSR* (London), 8 April 1974.
17.   Ibid.
18.   "A Statement from the Psychiatrist Gluzman, a Political Prisoner, to the Department of Administrative Organs of the CC CPSU" (16 June 1974) in *A Chronicle of Human Rights in the USSR*, Number 19, page 39.
19.   *Khronika Tekushchikh Sobitii*, Number 33, page 13.
20.   Ibid.

stomach removed because of an ulcer condition, Aleksander Sergiyenko suffers from chronic tuberculosis and Vladimir Bukovsky suffers from a duodenal ulcer and disorders of the heart and liver.

Transfer to an institution of a different regime represents a change in the prisoner's sentence. The exclusive right of courts to determine sentence is formally preserved by the requirement that only a court can order a long-term change in a prisoner's regime.[21] However, the MVD is apparently not prevented from using purely administrative methods to change prisoners' regime without recourse to the courts.

In 1972, 500 prisoners from colonies ZhKh 385/3, /17 and /19 in the Mordovian complex of colonies were transferred to two colonies in Perm. Some of those involved later stated that the reason for this large-scale transfer was "to redistribute the political camps, to prevent the flow of information, and to disrupt contacts among prisoners".[22] On arrival at the colonies VS 389/36 and VS 389/35, the prisoners were told that this entire zone was a "special corrective labour institution", meaning that the colonies in it are special regime colonies.[23] Since the prisoners were all serving strict regime sentences, the transfer represented a change in the regime to which they had been sentenced. This was illegal because not ordered by any court, but it was sanctioned by the MVD.

Apart from being in apparent violation of the law, this transfer of prisoners was carried out with infliction of much suffering on the prisoners involved.

> 15 people in a sleeping compartment. Everybody bathed in sweat. Food spoiled. For two days they did not take prisoners to the lavatory. People had to use the corridors . . . The windows were sealed shut. Only at the end of the deportation did they open the windows a little, but it did not help. People were lying naked on the floor. Dirt. Stink. Suffocating. One man died during the deportation. It was a terrible torture.[24]

Another account of the same journey confirms this description and adds:

> Even the smallest concession — a drop of water, a gulp of fresh air — could be gained only by collective screaming whenever the train was passing through a populated area. Some prisoners lost consciousness . . . Nikolai Nikolayenko was taken from the train to a hospital. No medical service was provided on the journey. Illiterate guards were indiscriminately handing out the same pills to everybody . . .[25]

The events described were a clear instance of the abuse by prison officials of their authority and of the defenceless position of the prisoners in their custody. Notwithstanding the legal principle that imprisonment in the USSR "shall not aim at inflicting physical suffering and degrading human dignity" prison authorities inflict suffering and degradation upon prisoners on a routine basis. In so doing they commit frequent violations of the letter of Soviet legislation.

In 1962, an article (77-1) was added to the RSFSR Criminal Code making the

21. *Commentary to the Fundamentals of Corrective Labour Legislation of the USSR and Union Republics* (1972), page 89.
22. "A Perm Camp" (1972-1973)
23. Ibid.
24. *Samizdat* document reproduced in *News Bulletin on Soviet Jewry* (Tel-Aviv), October 1972.
25. "A Perm Camp" (1972-1973).

death penalty the maximum sentence which a court could pass for "actions disrupting the work of corrective labour institutions". By many accounts this sentence was until recently imposed and executed very liberally for a variety of violations of discipline by prisoners. Edward Kuznetsov recalls that during his first term of imprisonment (from 1961 to 1968 after a conviction for "anti-Soviet agitation and propaganda") dozens of prisoners were executed in his Mordovian colony for tattooing anti-government slogans on their bodies or for self-mutilations of various kinds.[26] When he returned to a Mordovian colony (ZhKh 385/1) in 1971, he learned that in his absence executions for tattooing had been stopped.[27]

Although some colony administrations at least occasionally threaten prisoners with Article 77-1, the use of the death penalty in Soviet corrective labour institutions has clearly greatly decreased. Amnesty International knows of no case in recent years where a prisoner of conscience has been executed under Article 77-1.

In recent *samizdat* documents emanating from Soviet penal institutions, there are no cases recorded of such executions, either of political or of criminal prisoners.

Nonetheless the mere existence in law of the death penalty for violations of discipline by prisoners highlights the enormous discrepancy between the high moral claims of Soviet corrective labour law and the regime of intimidation to which the prisoners are permanently subjected.

## Legal Controls over Colony and Prison Administrations

The legal reforms which were enacted piecemeal in the USSR after 1953 were accompanied by efforts to restore the rule of law in Soviet prison institutions. Although new corrective labour codes were not legislated until 1970, already in the mid-1950s institutional changes were made providing legal supervision over colony and prison administrations. Most important was the 1955 Statute on the Supervisory Powers of the USSR Procuracy, which is still in effect. According to Article 35 of this statute, officers of the procuracy have an unlimited right to visit colonies and prisons to check documents related to prisoners' cases and to check the legality of all orders and directives of the administrations of corrective labour institutions. The same statute (in Article 36) calls for the procuracy to give timely consideration to complaints and petitions by prisoners. In addition, in 1957 public supervisory commissions were established throughout the USSR to act "as organs of public control over observance of legality in the activity of corrective labour institutions".[28]

In the present corrective labour legislation, the procuracy and public supervisory commissions are retained as the two channels for supervision of observance of legality in Soviet corrective labour institutions.

Article 11 of the RSFSR Corrective Labour Code stipulates that the USSR procuracy and its subordinate procuracies are to ensure "exact observance of the laws" in prison institutions. They are to prevent and punish violations of the law "from whomsoever these violations may emanate". In numerous places in

26.   Edward Kuznetsov, *Prison Diaries,* pages 165-167.
27.   Ibid, page 157.
28.   Natashev & Struchkov, ibid, page 58.

the code it is stated that the MVD (charged with administration of the prison system) is to cooperate with the procuracy in determining certain details of the operation of prisons and colonies. Article 11 of the RSFSR Corrective Labour Code also declares that prison administrations "are obliged to fulfil" the instructions of the procuracy regarding observation of the laws. To ensure that prisoners can bring abuses to the attention of the procuracy (and other organs and institutions), the Fundamentals of Corrective Labour Legislation assures them of the right to lodge complaints in writing.[29] According to the *Commentary to the Fundamentals of Labour Legislation of the USSR and Union Republics:*

> The right of convicted persons to make complaints is regarded as one of the important guarantees for provision of legality during the execution of punishment . . . The drawing up and sending of complaints is not limited by any norms whatever.[30]

However, prisoners' right to lodge complaints is generally abused. Only those letters of complaint sent by prisoners to the procuracy are exempt from obligatory censorship by the colony or prison administration.[31] This means that prisoners' complaints, unless addressed to the procuracy, are censored by the very officials who are the subjects of the complaints. This contravenes the Decree of the Presidium of the USSR Supreme Soviet of 12 April 1968 dealing with treatment of citizens' complaints. The decree states:

> It is forbidden to send convicted persons' complaints for decision by those official persons whose actions are the subject of the complaint.[32]

However, prisoners' complaints to ministries and other organizations are not only read by the colony or prison administration, but are often forwarded to the central corrective labour administration within the MVD.

Given the power which camp and prison administrations have to change conditions for any prisoner, they have considerable scope for taking revenge on prisoners who lodge complaints. Sometimes the process of revenge and intimidation is even given the appearance of legality, as the following account from a Perm colony illustrates:

> The camp administration informed the prisoners that there is a special instruction according to which the administration is authorized to censor prisoners' complaints and to decide whether they contain slander or whether they are objective. In the first case, that is if they find slander in the complaint, the camp administration has the right not to send on the complaint and the right to punish the prisoner for giving false information or for the presence of improper expressions in the letter. In this manner a number of prisoners were punished for sending complaints by punishment cell and by deprivation of parcels and visits.[33]

29. Fundamentals of Corrective Labour Legislation of the USSR and Union Republics Article 26.
30. *Commentary to the Fundamentals of Corrective Labour Legislation of the USSR and Union Republics* (1972), page 100.
31. Ibid, page 100. See also the anonymous *samizdat* document "About Instruction Number 020" (1974).
32. *Vedomosti Verkhovnogo Soveta SSSR,* Number 17, 1968.
33. "A Perm Camp" (1972-1973).

Even supposedly uncensored letters to the procuracy are of little avail, according to all accounts by Soviet prisoners of conscience. If the procuracy does involve itself in the situation inside colonies and prisons, it seems never to be on the side of the prisoners. This is well illustrated in the "diary" of the month-long hunger strike in Perm corrective labour colony VS 389/35 in the summer of 1974. The prisoners made numerous complaints about violations of law by the camp administration (for example, illegal withholding of mail and parcels, violation of the corrective labour code's articles on prisoners' labour, arbitrary deprival of visiting rights, violation of the norms regulating punishment of prisoners). The procuracy officials and all other agencies to which they appealed ignored these complaints. So convinced were the prisoners of the futility of complaining to the procuracy that many of them undertook a hunger strike, in spite of the fact that they were underfed and in many cases in poor health. When the prisoners again lodged complaints about further illegalities allegedly committed by the colony administration during the hunger strike, a high ranking official told them: "You can complain but you'd better learn that no procurator can help".[34]

After the hunger strike was over, the RSFSR procuracy examined complaints made by the hunger strikers against brutality and illegalities perpetrated by the colony's administration during the hunger strike. In August 1974, the colony's administration received from the RSFSR procuracy a formal letter rejecting each of the prisoners' complaints as "not proven" or "inconsistent with the facts".[35] That same month the Ukrainian writer Ivan Svitlichny formally challenged the procuracy's findings and again went on hunger strike. He was immediately put into a punishment cell for 3 months.[36]

The public supervisory commissions provide the second means of supervising the observance of legality in colonies. These supervisory commissions are attached to local soviets of workers' deputies at the region, city and district level. According to Article 110 of the RSFSR Corrective Labour Code, their membership is composed for the most part of "deputies of soviets and representatives of trade unions, Young Communists and other public organizations and workers' collectives". Workers of the MVD, procuracy and courts may not be members of the supervisory commissions.[37]

The supervisory commissions are legally entitled to concern themselves with all aspects of the functioning of corrective labour institutions. They are authorized to help in the re-education of prisoners. On the basis of their own evaluation of prisoners' records, they can seek early release of prisoners through the courts or their transfer from one type of regime ro another.[38]

The supervisory commissions are required to participate "in the implementation of public control" over the activity of corrective labour institutions.[39] To this end, they are endowed with broad rights to visit colonies and prisons to hear

34.  "The Journal of a Month-Long Hunger Strike" (1974).
35.  The procuracy's reply was signed by V. Bolysov, the RSFSR's chief inspector for corrective labour institutions.
36.  *Khronika Tekushchikh Sobitii,* Number 33, pages 27-28.
37.  *Ispravitel 'no Trudovoye Pravo* (1971), page 103.
38.  Ibid, page 106.
39.  RSFSR Corrective Labour Code, Article 110.

prisoners' complaints and to demand presentation of relevant documents by administrations.[40]

The gap between these legal provisions and practice is wide. To our knowledge, no supervisory commission has ever intervened on behalf of a Soviet prisoner of conscience adopted by Amnesty International, either by requesting his release or an easing in his conditions or by protesting violations of the law by colony or prison authorities. That the existence of the supervisory commissions is in practice irrelevant to political prisoners is attested to by the almost total absence of reference to the supervisory commissions in the large number of available statements and reports by and about prisoners of conscience in the USSR. The only substantial exception to this disregard for the supervisory commissions appeared in issue number 33 of *A Chronicle of Current Events*, which reported a supervisory commission's recommendation of early release for 8 prisoners in Mordovian colony ZhKh 385/19. Of the 8, 3 had been convicted of war crimes committed in collaboration with German occupation forces during World War II, two had served in the German occupation forces, one had given evidence against dissidents Pavel Litvinov and Larissa Bogoraz in 1969 and one, a former Latvian partisan, had only three months left to serve in a 10-year sentence.[41]

The Soviet jurist M.D. Shargorodsky wrote in 1973 that the view is still held tenaciously among the Soviet public that "the more severe the punishments applied the more effective will be the struggle with crime".[42] If in their operations the supervisory commissions reflect such views, this might be one explanation for their lack of effectiveness in the direction of easing prison conditions.

However, the public supervisory commissions do not operate independently of official organs. They are obliged to respect the principles and goals of the authorities charged with administering the prison system. Whatever the accuracy of Mr Shargorodsky's statement on Soviet public attitudes, the contemporary corrective labour legislation itself reflects a punitive, retributive understanding of imprisonment, and such an attitude is certainly characteristic of those who administer the application of that legislation. It is this attitude which determines the operations of the public supervisory commissions.

40. *Commentary to the Fundamentals of Corrective Labour Legislation of the USSR and Union Republics* (1972), pages 44-45.
41. *Khronika Tekushchikh Sobitii*, Number 33, page 17.
42. Shargorodsky, op.cit. page 49.

# Prisoners' States of Mind

Shukhov went to sleep, and he was very happy. He'd had a lot of luck today. They hadn't put him in the cooler. The gang hadn't been chased out to work in the Socialist Community Development. He'd finagled an extra bowl of mush at noon. The boss had gotten them good rates for their work. He'd felt good making that wall. They hadn't found that piece of steel in the frisk. Caesar had paid him off in the evening. He'd bought some tobacco. And he'd gotten over that sickness.

Nothing had spoiled the day and it had been almost happy.

There were three thousand six hundred and fifty-three days like this in his sentence, from reveille to lights out.

The three extra ones were because of the leap years.[1]

These were the thoughts of "Ivan Denisovich Shukhov" at the end of a day in a labour camp near the end of the Stalin era. They reflect the only honest means of survival which Alexander Solzhenitsyn could conceive for those who were faced with long years of imprisonment in a labour colony as he had been. Ivan Denisovich tried only to satisfy his elementary needs without stopping anyone else from doing so and never complained to officials or took chances which might make things worse.

There were and are other means of survival. Religious prisoners "escaped" from the brutality of prison life through prayers and faith. Many still do, and it has been remarked many times over the years that some of the hardiest and most upstanding inmates of Soviet prisons and colonies are devout religious believers.

Other prisoners find survival in debasement. Many prisoners seek favours from guards and administrators by spying on and informing on other prisoners. Edward Kuznetsov estimated in 1971 that out of 90 prisoners in his Mordovian colony 37 were informers and 7 others were suspected of being such.[2] Many criminal prisoners, especially, are enlisted to stage provocations involving political prisoners or even to beat and harass them. This report has already men-

---

1. Alexander Solzhenitsyn, *One Day in the Life of Ivan Denisovich* (Bantam Books, New York, 1963), pages 202-203. This work was first published in *Novy Mir* (Moscow), Number 11, 1962.
2. Edward Kuznetsov, *Prison Diaries*, page 213.

*Right:* Edward Kuznetsov

tioned the sustained assaults by criminal prisoners on Valentyn Moroz in 1972.[3]

Similar instances are common and will continue to be common as long as prison and colony authorities are willing to use their powers to dispense favours and disfavours as a cudgel against political prisoners as a particularly despised class of inmates.

When Alexander Solzhenitsyn and "Ivan Denisovich Shukhov" were serving their sentences, the Soviet prison world was totally isolated from human society outside the prisons. This was still true when Solzhenitsyn's *One Day in the Life of Ivan Denisovich* was published in the Soviet literary journal *Novy Mir* in 1962. As the authors of the "Introduction" to one English-language edition of the novel stated: "Solzhenitsyn has laid bare a whole new world",[4] a world which for many persons outside the USSR had not existed until Solzhenitsyn depicted it.

Since that time, the Soviet prisoner has become less isolated. It is not only the post-Stalin legislation of more human visiting and correspondence rights (frequently violated as they are) which has re-established some decree of contact between prisoner and society in the USSR. It is the emergence in recent years of a small, but not insignificant group of Soviet citizens anxious to plead openly the case of wrongfully-imprisoned persons, and the development of *samizdat* as a medium for this effort which have broken down the isolation of at least a part of the Soviet prison population. This change has brought with it a mode of survival for prisoners able to use it which was impossible 20 or even 10 years ago.

The importance of a mere attempt at communication with life outside the prison system was described by Edward Kuznetsov in relation to his *Prison Diaries:*

> I write only to stay human. This is a diabolical place, its purpose — to drive a man deeper and deeper into despair, to make him doubt whether truth after all is sacrosanct . . . A diary is for me a way of consciously opposing an impossible way of life. The very act of writing down the

3.  See above, page 46
4.  Max Hayward and Leopold Labedz, "Introduction" to Alexander Solzhenitsyn, *One Day in the Life of Ivan Denisovich* (Bantam Books, New York, 1963), page xiii.

features of prison camp existence, as it were, objectifies them, allows me to stand back and every so often stick my tongue out at them![5] Mr Kuznetsov, who is still serving his 15-year special regime sentence, by now knows that his *Prison Diaries* have circulated in *samizdat* within the USSR and in book form outside the country.

For prisoners of conscience like Mr Kuznetsov, articulation of convictions and experiences represents a means of surviving prison conditions without submitting to them. Imprisonment strengthens the politically dissident convictions of prisoners of conscience. Ukrainians, Jews, Balts, etc, imprisoned for protesting against nationalist discrimination, find greater discrimination in prison. Persons imprisoned for opposition to the influence of security organs in Soviet life find themselves at the disposal of MVD and KGB officers. Those convicted for demanding more exact adherence to legal and constitutional norms find greater illegality and arbitrariness inside penal institutions than outside.

Consequently many political prisoners continue their dissident activities during imprisonment. Many political prisoners exhaustively test all legal channels of protest against prison conditions. In this they probably do not differ from the majority of the prison population. However, they do not desist when such institutional approaches prove fruitless.

Especially in recent years, Soviet political prisoners have succeeded in communicating to the outside world much information about conditions in penal institutions and about their own activities. Despite the body searches of most visitors and of prisoners being released, there is a regular flow of written appeals, complaints, memoirs and oral information from the Perm and Mordovian colonies in particular. Many such documents circulate in *samizdat* in Moscow and elsewhere and figure in appeals and statements made available to non-Soviet press representatives in Moscow.

Possibly inspired by the massive work strikes which (unnoticed to most of the world) swept through the Siberian labour camps in the mid-1950s, political prisoners have adopted the hunger strike as the sole means of applying pressure to penal administrators for improvement of prison conditions. The widespread use of this method is especially remarkable in view of the hunger and malnutrition to which Soviet prisoners are subjected. By tradition, certain days (such as 5-10 December, the anniversary of the promulgation of the Soviet Constitution) are marked out for annual hunger strikes by Soviet political prisoners in whatever prison or colony they are held. Another example of the coordinated hunger strike occurred in 1974 when political prisoners in Mordovia and Perm chose 30 October as "Political Prisoners' Day" and marked the occasion by a one-day hunger strike.

Other hunger strikes are local in scope. This report has already alluded to the hunger strike in Perm colony VS 389/36 in May and June 1974. This hunger strike was planned to last for 31 days and initially had 25 participants. By the end of the 31 days, some 25 other prisoners had declared sympathy hunger strikes.[6]

Some hunger strikes are spontaneous. There are numerous cases in which a number of political prisoners have undertaken such action in defence of a

5.    Edward Kuznetsov, *Prison Diaries*, pages 120-121.
6.    "The Journal of a Month-Long Hunger Strike" (1974).

fellow-prisoner or in reaction against an official policy or action. Often individuals go on hunger strike alone as a protest against individual grievances.

Only occasionally do political prisoners' hunger strikes bring short-term benefits.[7] As a rule participants in hunger strikes are punished by deprivation of parcels and visits, confinement to punishment cells or transfer to more severe institutions such as Vladimir prison.

However, such activities, especially when part of the outside world notices, have an importance for prisoners' state of mind, even if they do not bring the concrete improvement in aid of which they were undertaken.

Hunger strikes and efforts to transmit information about prison and colony conditions also raise the level of confrontation with prison or colony authorities. The administrations are ill-disposed from the outset against political prisoners. The following observation by Valentyn Moroz has been corroborated in many first-hand accounts:

> Many political prisoners were shown criminal offenders and told: "They are thieves but they are our people. You are enemies".[8]

Political prisoners are persecuted on such grounds, and in return they challenge the administrators by more hunger strikes, appeals to outside opinion, etc. This in turn exacerbates the hostility of prison administrators towards political prisoners. The father of Yury Fedorov (sentenced in 1969 to 6 years' imprisonment for participation in a dissident Marxist group) reported after a visit to his son in Mordovian colony ZhKh 385/17 in 1972 that the colony's administrators "see anti-Soviet acts in literally any action by the prisoners".[9] The colony commandant G.P. Gorkushov told Mr Fedorov: "They are all bandits, and your son is the bandit of bandits."[10]

The intensification of the confrontation between political prisoners and prison officials explains in part the deterioration in certain aspects of Soviet prison conditions in recent years, as manifested for example in the 1972 MVD Instruction 020.[11] The more political prisoners protest and challenge official policies, the stronger are official reactions in the form of further persecutions of political prisoners. In this sense, political prisoners' continuation of their dissident activity within prison walls contributes to their own hardship and is a form of maladjustment to prison conditions.

However, harassment and persecution are not the worst penalties incurred by maladjustment to Soviet prison conditions. Many prisoners exposed to brutal and degrading conditions and lacking an "escape route" through religion or *samizdat* have been broken by Soviet prison life.

There are many recorded cases of convicts taking their own lives. For example in his Mordovian colony, Edward Kuznetsov saw several convicts invite death

7.  One exception was a hunger strike by Boris Azernikov, Kronid Lyubarsky and Boris Penson in Mordovian colony ZhKh 385/19 in June 1974. After their week-long hunger strike, the three men suddenly received a backlog of letters which had previously been held back from them. See *Khronika Tekushchikh Sobitii*, Number 32, page 43.

8.  Valentyn Moroz, "A report from the Beria Reservation", in *Boomerang: The Works of Valentyn Moroz*, page 49.

9.  Letter by I.F. Fyodorov to USSR Procurator General R. Rudenko (21 May 1972). in *A Chronicle of Human Rights in the USSR*, Number 2, 1973.

10. Ibid.

11. See above, page 83.

by feigning escape attempts in full view of armed guards.[12] Anatoly Marchenko described such suicidal "escape attempts" as "putting an end to oneself in the usual way, that is with the help of the sentries".[13] Other suicide attempts are by more conventional methods. In Perm colony VS 398/36 in 1974, the prisoner Opanasenko hanged himself and left a note saying: "No more strength to hold out. Curse you, monsters!"[14]

Mr Openasenko's case was typical in that he had served 22 years of a 25-year sentence.

Another type of manifestation of breakdown of prisoners in Soviet penal institutions is self-mutilation. Reports of the most horrible instances of this phenomenon have aroused scepticism among some observers outside the USSR. Self-mutilation is not a typical response by prisoners. However, there are many recorded instances and the occurance of this practice cannot be dismissed. Indeed, self-mutilation has even been used collectively.

Issue Number 24 of *A Chronicle of Current Events* reported that in March 1972, 15 prisoners in an ordinary regime colony "sewed up their mouths" in protest against conditions in the colony. Some of the prisoners involved were immediately sent to the Leningrad special psychiatric hospital, and others were placed in punishment cells. The commandant of the colony was dismissed.[15] The following issue of *A Chronicle of Current Events* reported that many of those sent to punishment cells were again "inflicting injuries on themselves" and had therefore been "chained with handcuffs whose construction prevents any movement of the hands" to prevent self-mutilations and attacks on guards.[16]

Edward Kuznetsov wrote in 1971 that during two prison terms in Mordovian colonies he had seen many such incidents:

> I have many times witnessed some of the most fantastic incidences of self-mutilation. I have seen convicts swallow huge numbers of nails and quantities of barbed wire; I have seen them swallow mercury thermometers, pewter tureens (after first breaking them up into "edible" proportions), chess pieces, dominoes, needles, ground glass, spoons, knives and many other similar objects; I have seen convicts sew up their mouths and eyes with thread or wire; sew rows of buttons to their bodies; or nail their testicles to a bed, swallow a nail bent like a hook, and then attach this hook to the door by way of a thread so that the door cannot be opened without pulling the 'fish' inside out. I have seen convicts cut open the skin on their arms and legs and peel it off as if it were a stocking; or cut out lumps of flesh (from their stomach or their legs), roast them and eat them; or let the blood drip from a slit vein into a tureen, crumble bread crumbs into it, and then gulp it dpwn like a bowl of soup; or cover themselves with paper and set fire to themselves; or cut off their fingers, or their nose, or ears, or penis . . .[17]

12.  Edward Kuznetsov, *Prison Diaries*, pages 152-153.
13.  Anatoly Marchenko, *My Testimony*, page 94, pages 277-281.
14.  Reported in "The Journal of a Month-Long Hunger Strike" (1974).
15.  *A Chronicle of Current Events*, Number 24, page 144. A number of similar cases are recorded in Anatoly Marchenko, *My Testimony*, pages 78-79, pages 139-142, pages 314-316.
16   *A Chronicle of Current Events*, Number 25, page 204.
17.  Edward Kuznetsov, *Prison Diaries*, page 169.

Mr Kuznetsov attempted to explain this phenomenon. For him the persons who engaged in self-mutilation were not, as they are often presented, "tragic victims of the regime, its hunted and its persecuted".

> Many of these people are masochists, in a permanent state of depression from one blood-letting to the next. Many of them display symptoms of degeneracy (the pain-resistant level of their skin, for example, is lower than normal) . . . The destructive element within them boils over in a rage of impotence and is transformed into fits of hatred and feverish dreams of revenge on the prison governor; as soon as they realize that they can't get their teeth into his throat, they finally turn on themselves.[18]

Anatoly Marchenko witnessed such incidents both in Mordovian colonies and in Vladimir prison. He became accustomed to it.

> What had I been reduced to by a few months in prison! . . . Now I could greedily swallow my sprat in the midst of blood and vomit and it seemed to me that there was nothing in the world tastier than that sprat of mine. A man pours out his blood before my eyes and I lick my soup bowl clean and think only about how long it is till the next meal. Did anything human remain in me, or in any of us, in that prison?[19]

These lines represent Soviet conditions of imprisonment in their worst aspect, and it may be unfair to end on such a note. Perhaps some prisoners in Soviet corrective labour institutions, and even some prisoners of conscience, develop attitudes which correspond more closely to the officially-proclaimed goals of imprisonment. They are the exception rather than the rule.

18.    Ibid, page 170.
19.    Anatoly Marchenko, *My Testimony*, page 151.

# Compulsory Detention in Psychiatric Hospitals

In 1960, the Soviet writer and literary critic Valery Tarsis sent abroad for publication a work called *The Bluebottle,* in which he criticized a number of aspects of modern Soviet life. In August 1962, shortly before this work was published abroad for the first time (in England), Valery Tarsis was arrested and confined to a psychiatric hospital in Moscow. Much foreign publicity ensued, and in March 1963 he was released. The following year he sent abroad for publication *Ward 7,* a thinly-veiled autobiographical account of his experiences with Soviet psychiatry.[1] In 1966, Valery Tarsis emigrated from the USSR.

In January 1970, Vladimir Bukovsky was released following 3 years of imprisonment for having taken part in a demonstration in Moscow's Pushkin Square in 1967. Mr Bukovsky had already in the mid-1960s spent around 20 months in psychiatric hospitals after being arrested for possessing copies of Milovan Djilas' book *The New Class.* For over a year after his release in 1970, Mr Bukovsky devoted much effort to compiling documentation on the psychiatric diagnosis and treatment of political dissenters in the USSR. He gave interviews (including a televised one) on the subject to foreign correspondents.

In early 1971, Mr Bukovsky sent to the West a collection of materials documenting abuses of psychiatry in the USSR.[2] In January 1971, he appealed to Western psychiatrists to study the question and to come out in defence of Soviet victims of psychiatric abuse. In March 1971, he was arrested.

In January 1972, Vladimir Bukovsky was tried. Among the specific charges was his having communicated to foreign correspondents "slanderous" assertions that in the USSR healthy persons have been confined to special psychiatric hospitals. He was found guilty of "anti-Soviet agitation and propaganda" and sentenced to 2 years in prison, 5 years in a strict regime corrective labour colony, and 5 years in exile.

If after Valery Tarsis' release from psychiatric hospital in 1963 there was a long hiatus in world interest in the relationship between politics and psychiatry

1.   Valery Tarsis, *Ward 7* (Collins-Harvill, London, 1965).
2.   These documents were published in French in V. Boukovsky (editor), *Une nouvelle maladie mentale en URSS: l'opposition* (Seuil, Paris, 1971), and in German in W. Bukowski (editor), *Opposition: Eine neue Geisteskrankheit in der Sowjetunion?* Carl Hanser Verlag, Munich, 1972).

*Above:* Semyon Gluzman     *Above:* Vladimir
                                             Gershuni     *Above:* Vladimir Bukovsky

*Below:* The family of Leonid Plyushch: son
            Dima, wife Tatyana Zhitnikova, son Lesik.     *Below:* Leonid Plyushch

*Below:* General Pyotr Grigorenko and his wife Zinaida, taken
            in October 1974 several months after his release
            from a psychiatric hospital.

in the USSR, this has not been true of the period since Vladimir Bukovsky's publicity efforts in 1970 and 1971. Since that time, many non-Soviet psychiatrists jurists, human rights organizations and representatives of the media have devoted considerable energy to investigating and publicizing cases like those described by Mr Bukovsky. They have had much material to work with. Inspired by Mr Bukovsky and encouraged by foreign interest, many inmates and ex-inmates of Soviet psychiatric hospitals, and their friends, relatives and sympathizers, have written about their experiences in appeals, open letters and memoirs, or spoken about the subject in personal and telephone conversations with non-Soviet citizens. Some of these people have left the USSR and given further testimony on arriving outside the country.

In the face of widespread criticism of political abuses of psychiatry, Soviet authorities have countered with denials and by putting the criticism down to "anti-Soviet" sentiments both within the USSR and abroad. In so doing, they have been more forthcoming with information about detention on psychiatric grounds than they have ever been about regular forms of imprisonment, and have contributed to the stock of information needed in evaluating allegations that healthy persons have been (and are) committed against their will to psychiatric hospitals for political reasons.

The controversy is a deeply emotional one. On the one side stand the "victims": persons who in connection with their non-conformist political and religious views have been at one time or another declared "insane" and who often have been subjected to "total" efforts at medical "treatment" completely against their will. Such individuals and persons close to them are likely to be bitter to a degree even greater than political inmates of ordinary penal institutions. In evaluating the evidence given by such persons it is necessary to take into account not only their moral indignation and bitterness but the fact that they usually avoid giving testimony which could be officially interpreted to justify the practices they condemn. The fear that minor concessions could be distorted is justified, in view of a number of cases in which Soviet media have misinterpreted statements on Soviet psychiatry by visiting non-Soviet psychiatrists.[3]

On the other side stand Soviet authorities, anxious to preserve the image of Soviet science in public service and faced with disgrace by allegations of willful and vicious use of medicine for political repression. Such authorities have no choice but to deny all allegations of abuse of psychiatry in their country.

Yet the evidence is not as polarized as might appear at first glance. Much of the material which represents the official point of view supports the accusations levelled at Soviet psychiatry. A study of the legal provisions which relate to compulsory confinement on psychiatric grounds makes plain the opportunity for abuse of psychiatry either out of negligence or by design. Public pronouncements by leading representatives of Soviet psychiatry reveal the dominance in their work of criteria for mental illness which are so loosely formulated as to bring into the province of psychiatry any manifestation of dissent on public issues.

3.   Reportage of such cases can be found in Anthony de Meeus, *Livre Blanc sur l'internement psychiatrique de dissidents sains d'esprit en URSS* (Comite International Pour la Defense des Droits de l'Homme en URSS: Brussels, 1974), pages 57-60.

Of telling importance is the fact that official and public Soviet statements in reaction to allegations of abuse of psychiatry in the USSR have never come to grips with the specific content of those allegations. For example, there has been no official Soviet reaction to frequent reference by critics to a number of "official psychiatric diagnoses" of political dissidents.[4] These documents are of deep importance. Each of them served as the official basis for compulsory confinement of a political dissident to a psychiatric hospital. They are so rich in decisive evidence supporting allegations of political abuse of psychiatry in the USSR as to make the question of their authenticity vital.

Were these documents counterfeit, presumably Soviet authorities would declare them to be such. This has never happened. Moreover, if the documents genuinely are official psychiatric diagnoses, and if the psychiatric method displayed in them is officially approved, any false claims denouncing these documents as forgeries would undercut the work done by Soviet psychiatrists at the behest (direct or indirect) of state agencies. This may only be part of the explanation for the refusal of Soviet authorities to denounce these documents as forgeries. The failure to so dismiss them remains an argument in favour of accepting them as genuine — but not the only such argument.

The available official psychiatric diagnoses outside the USSR and the large amount of written and spoken evidence given by concerned parties in support of allegations of political abuses of Soviet psychiatry stand up to close scrutiny. The numerous separate individual accounts, usually made by persons who do not know one another, are mutually corroborative on even minor details. The general picture which emerges from such accounts is coherent and cannot be dismissed as fiction or as the result of a coordinated effort at distortion of reality.

On the basis of the available documentary evidence, Amnesty International accepts as fact the general allegation that numerous Soviet citizens have been confined to psychiatric hospital as a direct result of their political or religious beliefs and with no medical justification.

Any attempt to estimate the number of persons so confined meets obstacles even greater than those encountered in estimating the numbers of political and religious prisoners detained in ordinary prison institutions.[5] The main additional obstacle is that inmates of special psychiatric hospitals (where most "political" inmates are held) are kept in even greater isolation from the outside world than prisoners in corrective labour institutions.

Secondly, once interned in a special psychiatric hospital, a person can be kept there indefinitely ("pending recovery") and virtually disappear from society. The difficulty this imposes for estimating the number of "political" inmates of psychiatric hospitals is compounded by the fact that the history of this phenomenon did not begin in the early 1970s, when large amounts of documentary evidence on the subject began to emerge from the USSR, or even in 1962, when

4.   In 1972 a number of such documents were entered in evidence to a United States Congressional committee investigating this subject, and were published (among other places) in *Abuse of Psychiatry for Political Repression in the Soviet Union* (US Government Printing Office, Washington, 1972).

5.   See above, pages 50-53.

the world media devoted great attention to the confinement of writer Valery Tarsis to a psychiatric hospital for his highly critical writings.

In 1955-56, on the initiative of party member S.P. Pisarev, the Central Comcittee of the Communist Party of the Soviet Union created a special commission to investigate allegations of repressive misuse of psychiatry.[6] According to Mr Pisarev, this commission discovered that "year after year" psychiatry had been systematically abused as a device for incarcerating mentally healthy persons.

It listed systematically the perversions of truth in the diagnoses by the Serbsky Institute, in particular by D.R. Lunts (at that time a senior lecturer) and a number of other people. It was documentarily proved that, through the fault of the diagnostic institute under investigation, Soviet psychiatric hospitals throughout the country, and above all the two notorious special prisons for political prisoners in Kazan and Leningrad, had year after year been filled up by sane persons . . . who had been the *innocent sufferers* and victims of illegal repressive measures.[7]

This officially-sponsored report was suppressed. According to Mr Pisarev, some improvements were subsequently made in the special psychiatric hospitals.[8] Nonetheless, the total number of special psychiatric hospitals has more than doubled since the time of the commission, and the abuse of psychiatry for political purposes has continued.

Amnesty International knows in some detail the cases of about 120 Soviet citizens who have been confined by court order to psychiatric hospitals for political or religious reasons since January 1969. This figure does not include those who have been sent for prolonged diagnosis (rather than "treatment") in psychiatric institutes. Nor does it include the undefined number of inmates of ordinary penal institutions who have been held in psychiatric wards in those institutions and about whose cases little information is available. Finally, many of those Soviet citizens who have written accounts of their experiences in psychiatric hospitals have mentioned in passing other persons who had been placed there on account of their political beliefs or activities. This in itself supports the view that the number of such persons on whom substantial documentation is available outside the USSR is only a fraction of the total.

## The Background

Since 1917, a great deal of attention has been given in the USSR to development of the relationship between psychiatry and the law. This was especially encouraged in the first decade of Soviet power by radical trends in Soviet jurisprudence which attempted to locate the cause of crime not in individual guilt but in the social-economic evils of pre-socialist society.[9] In this situation psychiatrists were influential in the creation of legal measures for the protection of persons from the legal consequences of crimes committed while in a state of

6.   Letter by S.P. Pisarev to the USSR Academy of Medical Sciences (20 April 1970), reproduced in *Survey* (London), Number 77, Autumn 1970, pages 176-177.
7.   Ibid, pages 177.
8.   Ibid, page 178.
9.   Where political "crime" was concerned, a wholly different philosophy was dominant according to which an individual could be convicted under criminal law even if it was known that he had committed no crime: 1926 RSFSR Criminal Code, Article 7.

mental illness, whether chronic or temporary. Thus, Article 11 of the 1926 RSFSR Criminal Code stipulated that while social defence measures and medical treatment could be applied to such persons, they could not be punished under criminal law. In 1922, the Serbsky Institute of Forensic Psychiatry was founded in Moscow with the task of researching the relationship between mental illness and crime so as "to protect the rights of persons with unbalanced minds who might commit acts dangerous to society not with an evil intention but involuntarily."[10]

Until the mid-1930s, psychiatrists' findings were used in a very liberal manner to free numerous persons from criminal responsibility. However, when the experimental trends in Soviet jurisprudence came into official disapproval and the concept of individual guilt for crime was reasserted, the influence of medical opinion on criminal court decisions was greatly reduced. Nonetheless, psychiatric criteria continued to serve as a means of gaining asylum for mentally ill persons and for some who were not mentally ill. As Alexander Yesenin-Volpin pointed out in an "expert opinion" prepared for the Moscow Human Rights Committee, psychiatrists have used diagnoses of "mental illness" as a means of protecting people from political repression.

... during the widespread Stalinist repressions many persons were saved by psychiatric hospitals, and, whatever the present situation, one must not forget this.[11]

The present Soviet criminal codes retain the principle that mentally ill persons cannot be subjected to punishment for crimes they may have committed.[12]

The notion that Soviet psychiatric hospitals still offer asylum, according to a number of contemporary sources, brings some convicted criminals to try to obtain false psychiatric diagnoses which will effect their transfer from corrective labour institutions to mental hospital. (The same reports usually add that after a brief stay in special psychiatric hospitals, such persons regret this move, for reasons which will be described below.)

The development in Soviet law of measures protecting mentally ill persons has been impelled by humanitarian motives and has been presented by at least one non-Soviet authority as "a long step toward the solution of an age-old conflict between the standards of medical science and the requirements of an effective legal order".[13]

Yet this is only one part of the picture. When a Soviet court is informed by expert opinion that a defendant is mentally ill and releases him from criminal responsibility and from subjection to punishment, it also must order measures which will protect society from further harmful actions by the defendant. Among the actions which may be and often are ordered by Soviet courts in such cases are compulsory confinement and compulsory medical treatment.

10.    Radio Moscow Czech-language broadcast, 10 October 1973. Translated and published by the Monitoring Service of the British Broadcasting Corporation, 12 October 1973.
11.    A. Yesenin-Volpin, "Mneniye Eksperta Komiteta Prav Cheloveka", in *Proceedings of the Moscow Human Rights Committee* (International League for the Rights of Man,• New York, 1972), page 135.
12.    RSFSR Criminal Code, Article 11.
13.    Harold J. Berman, *Justice in the USSR: An Interpretation of Soviet Law* (Harvard University Press, Cambridge, Massachusetts, 1963), page 314.

This aspect of the relationship between psychiatry and law has many times and in many countries entailed the most gross and inhumane abuses against individuals. These abuses consist in their being incarcerated with no conscious hope of release, and in their being medically treated in a manner not of their own choice but reflecting at best the local state of medical knowledge at the given time.

Psychiatrists and jurists in many countries have recognized that in cases of confinement of persons to mental hospitals against their will, there are real dangers that the intolerance or ignorance of persons in authority may take precedence over the need of the patient for treatment or the need of society for protection. It is widely recognized that these dangers must be countered by continuous improvement of psychiatric service and, even more so, by development in law of powerful procedural rights for all persons deprived of the right to judge for themselves the propriety of their own behaviour.

Yet highly placed and authoritative representatives of the Soviet psychiatric profession have publicly and unequivocally rejected from consideration any need for development of stronger barriers in the USSR against abuses perpetrated against individuals whose place in society is challenged on psychiatric grounds. For example, in August 1973 Dr A.V. Snezhnevsky, a member of the USSR Academy of Sciences and a leading psychiatrist at Moscow's Serbsky Institute of Forensic Psychiatry, was called upon to put paid to claims that Soviet psychiatry has been abused for political purposes. Dr Snezhnevsky said that "in 50 years of work in the Soviet publis health service he knew of no case in which a healthy man was put in a psychiatric hospital".[14] This statement, frequently repeated by Dr Snezhnevsky and other leading Soviet psychiatrists, is simply not credible. It conflicts with common sense, and there is no country in the world in which such optimistic self-praise could truthfully be made. Moreover, such Soviet claims are further countered by numerous well-documented allegations of specific errors and politically motivated abuses in psychiatric practice in the USSR.[15] Finally, a close examination of the currently operative Soviet laws governing compulsory detention on psychiatric grounds makes clear that, contrary to official Soviet claims, those laws do not contain sufficient guarantees against the abuse of psychiatry for wrongful detention and harmful treatment of individuals.

On the basis of the character of the relevant Soviet legal norms and judging from certain peculiarities of psychiatric judgement exhibited in available forensic psychiatric diagnoses, it appears probable that wrongful detention of citizens on psychiatric grounds but without political motivation is as common in the USSR as elsewhere. One former Soviet citizen has said:

> The problem would be artificially simplified if one were to speak only of persecutions for ideological dissent. We should also mention the violations of the rights of thousands of people labelled mentally ill for other kinds of behaviour (not necessarily ideological). Their rights are sometimes violated entirely without objection. Sometimes they are violated with

14. *Isvestiya*, 31 August 1973.
15. Many documents used by Amnesty International as evidence of such abuses have been collected by the United States Senate Committee on the Judiciary and published under the title *Abuses of Psychiatry for Political Repression in the Soviet Union* (US Government Printing Office, Washington DC, 1972).

the help of mercenary (or merely weary) relatives who either do not want to or cannot try to defend those rights.[16]

However, because Amnesty International's task is to work for prisoners of conscience, and because the available documentation is written by or about victims of politically motivated abuse of psychiatry, it is on such cases that this report will concentrate.

## Soviet Law and Psychiatry

In most cases known to Amnesty International of Soviet citizens' being confined to psychiatric hospitals because of their political or religious views, the procedure used has been that provided by criminal law.[17] Soviet criminal legislation stipulates that if officials investigating a criminal case question the mental health of the accused, they must request a psychiatric diagnosis of him by a psychiatric commission. If this commission declares that the accused is suffering from mental illness or was mentally incapacitated at the time of his alleged commission of the crime, criminal charges must be dropped and the diagnosis presented to a court. The court then decides whether to relieve the accused of criminal responsibility and order him to be confined for "compulsory measures of a medical character".

As was mentioned earlier in this report, the drafters of the present criminal legislation, motivated by the excessive illegalities of the Stalin period, included in the law much stronger formal guarantees of the procedural rights of persons accused of criminal offences.[18] In several places, the criminal legislation implies that such procedural guarantees apply to accused persons whose mental health is called into question. However, such cases are formally distinguished from regular cases by the dedication to them of a separate chapter in each republic's criminal procedure code. (In the RSFSR Code of Criminal Procedure, it is chapter 33). Official commentaries on these codes make clear that the investigation and judicial consideration of such cases are distinguished by "specific peculiarities".[19] To be exact, the procedural rights of persons suspected of being mentally ill are simplified, and in such a way as to leave them with almost no rights other than the passive right to an honest examination and an honest hearing.

Articles 184 and 185 of the RSFSR Code of Criminal Procedure grant to an accused person broad rights to challenge during the investigation period the methods and findings of any forensic commission called upon to offer an expert opinion on his case. Article 188 specifically extends these rights to persons subjected to forensic psychiatric examination. However, Article 188 is rendered

---

16. Valery Chalidze, *To Defend These Rights: Human Rights and the Soviet Union* (Random House, New York, 1975), page 146.
17. The most graphic account of abuses of the civil procedure for compulsory confinement on psychiatric grounds is that by Zhores and Roy Medvedev, *A Question of Madness* (Penguin Books, London, 1971).
18. We have indicated in the first sections of this report that such formal rights are liable to be neglected or abused in cases with political ramifications.
19. See for example L.N. Smirnov (editor), *Nauchno-Praktichesky Kommentarii K Ugolovnomu-Protsessualnomu Kodeksu RSFSR* (Moscow, 1970), page 518. Hereafter this title will be referred to in English: *Scientific-Practical Commentary to the RSFSR Code of Criminal Procedure* (1970).

meaningless by a paragraph in Article 184 which states that, if it has been decided to submit an accused person to a psychiatric examination, he need not be informed of the psychiatric commission's opinion, or even of the fact that his mental health has been called into question.

Even before any court has seen a psychiatric commission's findings on an accused person's state of mind, he is excluded from participation in the investigation of his case. The investigation officials need not inform him of new charges against him or show him any documentation compiled on his case, and "as a rule" he is denied such rights.[20]

According to Soviet law, trials must be open except in certain types of cases involving state secrets, sex crimes, etc. In overtly political trials, special measures are required if the authorities wish to prevent the broad public from attending or learning about such trials.[21] In many republics of the USSR, such measures are not necessary if the sanity of the accused person is brought into question. For example, in the RSFSR there is no requirement that such hearings be held in public. One official commentary on the RSFSR Code of Criminal Procedure has criticized "those courts which hear all cases of this category in closed session".[22] However, there is no doubt that any court in the RSFSR has the option of closing the court in such hearings, and that in cases of persons accused of political "crimes", court hearings are held *in camera*. In the Ukraine, by contrast, such hearings must by law be open to the public. (However, in that republic judges too often hold hearings of such political cases in secrecy.)

According to Article 407 of the RSFSR Code of Criminal Procedure, it is left to the discretion of the court whether to allow the accused person to appear at the court hearing which decides on the validity of an expert diagnosis of his state of mind. Nor has the accused any legal right to send a written statement to the court hearing. Article 407 does not even mention the possible presence of the accused's immediate relatives at such a hearing, although relatives are among the categories of persons who may at the court's discretion be allowed to act as "legal representative" of the accused.[23] An official commentary on the same code states that the presence of the accused's relatives might be "useful", but makes clear that this, too, is at the court's discretion.[24]

In one of the very few explicit procedural guarantees for persons whose mental health is called into question, the law states that participation of a defence attorney is "mandatory" in court hearings of such cases.[25] This requirement is presumably intended to compensate for the fact that such accused persons do not have any legal possibility to defend themselves. Yet this article apparently does not require defence counsel to meet his client. For example, Valeria Novodvorskaya, a 19-year-old student who was diagnosed "mentally ill" after being arrested in late 1969 for distributing leaflets critical of the Communist

20.  *Scientific-Practical Commentary to the RSFSR Code of Criminal Procedure* (1970), p. 520.
21.  See above, pages 32-35.
22.  *Scientific-Practical Commentary to the RSFSR Code of Criminal Procedure* (1970), p.508.
23.  RSFSR Code of Criminal Procedure, Article 405.
24.  *Scientific-Practical Commentary to the RSFSR Code of Criminal Procedure* (1970), p.522.
25.  RSFSR Code of Criminal Procedure, Article 405.

110

Party, never met her advocate Dobuzhsky.[26] Hers was not an isolated example of this phenomenon. It is difficult to conceive how a defence counsel can defend against criminal charges and a psychiatric diagnosis without having met his client.

The court need not even inform the purportedly mentally ill defendant of the date or occurrence of the court hearing of his case. Valeria Novodvorskaya was declared mentally ill and ordered to be confined to the Kazan special psychiatric hospital without being informed of her hearing, and this too is a common occurrence.[27]

Vasily Chernyshov, a Leningrad intellectual declared insance in 1970 after being charged with "anti-Soviet agitation and propaganda", described the process by which he was ordered to be confined to a psychiatric hospital:

> In prison I was examined for 30 minutes and this diagnosis was made: chronic schizophrenia of a paranoid type. I did not meet my defence counsel, was not present at my trial, and for 1½ months did not even know about the diagnosis or the trial. It was my wife who, after the trial, told me about it when she visited me. She represented me at the trial, but had not been informed of the nature of the case — a flagrant breach of the law.[28]

## Politics, Psychiatry and the Courts

The authors of the present Soviet criminal laws no doubt justified the absence of stringent procedural guarantees by the expectation that justice and the rights of purportedly mentally ill accused persons would be protected at two decisive instances: the psychiatrists' formulation of their diagnosis and the final judgement of the court.

Soviet criminal legislation requires that any forensic psychiatric examination has as its purpose the supplying of an independent, objective and expert opinion on the facts of the case under investigation.[29] Soviet authorities and leading figures in the field of forensic psychiatry often emphasize that it is within the framework of the Soviet public health service and under the aegis of the Ministries of Public Health that forensic psychiatric examinations are conducted. Soviet authorities further support the claim that forensic psychiatric commissions are conducted independently by noting that Soviet psychiatrists, who are bound by professional oath, are criminally responsible if they wilfully advance a wrong diagnosis.[30]

In law and in practice, the conduct of expert psychiatric diagnoses is open to influence originating not only in the Ministries of Public Health but in the state security and police organs. It is the investigation officials who decide in the first instance to submit an accused person for psychiatric examination, and who decide which experts or expert institution shall conduct the examination.[31] It is the same

26. Valery Chalidze, *To Defend These Rights,* page 144; see "Notes from Soviet Asylums", *The National Review,* 9 June 1972, page 6.
27. Ibid, page 6.
28. "The Case of Vassily I Chernyshov", in *Abuse of Psychiatry for Political Repression in the Soviet Union,* page 225.
29. See RSFSR Code of Criminal Procedure, Articles 178-194.
30. See, for example, a Radio Moscow Czech-language broadcast, 10 October 1973, in BBC *Summary of World Broadcasts.*
31. RSFSR Code of Criminal Procedure, Article 184.

*Above:* Dr Georgy Morozov

investigation officials who decide "the questions placed before the expert and the materials made available to the expert".[32] In ordinary criminal cases the investigation officials may be officers of the procuracy, the institution which also conducts the prosecution of the case. In cases with political aspects, the KGB or the MVD, or both, assist in the investigation and call upon particular psychiatrists to contribute to their investigation.

According to Professor Georgy Morozov, head of the Serbsky Institute, the fact that a forensic psychiatric commission is composed of several psychiatrists provides reasonable assurance that the commission's work will be "objective".[33] It must be emphasized that this provision has not served to preserve the independence or objectivity of forensic psychiatric commissions in political cases. Greater objectivity would be obtained if at least one of the examining psychiatrists were nominated by the accused or by his relatives, a right formally extended to accused persons confronted with other types of expert forensic commissions by Article 185 of the RSFSR Code of Criminal Procedure. However, as has been stated by Zhores Medvedev, a prominent scientist who was compulsorily admitted to an ordinary psychiatric hospital in 1970 and released only after widespread public protest:

> In practice the psychiatric team for political cases is selected by the prosecution and the administrators of psychiatric institutions. In most cases the nomination of such teams is the responsibility of G. Morozov, Director

32.  Ibid.
33.  Georgy Morozov, "Soviet Forensic Psychiatry", *Anglo-Soviet Journal,* October, 1972.

of Serbsky Institute of Forensic Psychiatry. Psychiatrists recommended by lawyers or relatives have never been incorporated into such teams.[34]

The expert psychiatrists officially called into the case are in the employ of the Soviet state. This in itself leaves them open to suggestion from state authorities with a vested interest in political cases. That influence is liable to be direct and difficult to resist. Like other Soviet state institutions psychiatric institutions, or at least the larger ones, include in their "First Section" representatives of the KGB.

The Serbsky Institute, which according to its director Georgy Morozov "comes under the Ministry of Public Health",[35] seems to have particularly strong connections with the security organs. This was affirmed as long ago as 1955 and 1956 by the commission which was authorized by the Central Committee of the Communist Party of the Soviet Union (CPSU) to investigate alleged abuse of psychiatry.[36] More recently a number of Soviet dissidents examined in the Serbsky Institute have commented on the KGB's strong presence in that institution. Thus, Pyotr Grigorenko wrote at the end of the 1960s:

> This institution is nominally in the system of the USSR Ministry of Health, but I personally and more than once have seen Professor Lunts, the head of the department in which my diagnosis was drawn up, coming to work in the uniform of a KGB colonel. True, when he came into the department he always wore a white coat. I saw other doctors of this institution in KGB uniform as well. I haven't succeeded in ascertaining the exact relationship between these KGB officers and the Ministry of Health.
>
> People say that only one department is under the KGB — the department which conducts expert diagnoses in political cases. I personally think that the KGB's influence, which is the decisive influence, extends over all the institute's work. But even if things are as people say they are, the question arises: can a psychiatric expert diagnosis in a political case be objective if the investigator and the expert are subordinate to one and the same person, and even tied to one another by military discipline?[37]

The KGB is an extremely powerful institution, a fact attested to by the membership of its chairman, Yury Andropov, in the Politburo of the Central Committee of the CPSU and by innumerable first-hand accounts by Soviet citizens. Given the strong presence of the KGB in the Serbsky Institute, and its direct role in invoking psychiatric diagnoses in political cases, it would be very surprising indeed if the KGB's influence were not in some way reflected in such diagnoses.

Even if, as is extremely doubtful, the KGB does not have a direct influence on some psychiatrists, it is beyond dispute that Soviet forensic psychiatrists are bound to judge many individuals' political views with a view to determining their

34. *Nature* (London), Volume 244, 24 August 1973, page 477.
35. Georgy Morozov, "Soviet Forensic Psychiatry", *Anglo-Soviet Journal,* October 1972, page 64.
36. S.P. Pisarev, letter to the Presidium of the USSR Academy of Medical Sciences, 20 April 1970. The full text of this letter is reproduced in *Survey* (London), Number 77, Autumn 1970.
37. Pyotr Grigorenko, "O Spetsial'nykh Psikhiatriches kikh Bol'nitsakh ('Durdomakh')", in *Myslyi Sumasshedshego: Izbrannye Pisma i Vystupleniya Petra Griogoriyevicha Grigorenko* (Amsterdam, Herzen Foundation, 1973), page 234.

state of mental health. This follows inevitably from the inclusion in the law[38] of such articles as 70 ("anti-Soviet agitation and propaganda") and 190-1 ("Circulation of Fabrications known to be False Which Defame the Soviet State and Social System"). These loosely-worded articles make criminal a wide range of political (or religious) utterances. Any Soviet citizen who, exercising his constitutuional right to "freedom of speech", criticizes a sensitive aspect of official policy (for example, the 1968 occupation of Czechoslovakia) is liable to arrest and prosecution.

If for whatever reason the officials investigating his case decide to submit him to psychiatric examination, forensic psychiatrists must examine his "crime" (political utterances officially deemed "anti-Soviet" or "slanderous") just as they would have in other cases to examine crimes such as rape, murder or arson. The examining psychiatrists must judge the political utterances of the accused, not according to the ordinary criteria of debate and credibility, but against official norms of behaviour which have already proscribed the accused's political views by making their utterance grounds for arrest. The specific task of the examining psychiatrists is to recommend answers to the questions: were the accused's political utterances (and his political views) a consequence of mental illness, and is he likely to persist in proclaiming proscribed political opinions? If the answer to both these questions is "yes", then Soviet forensic psychiatrists are required by law to recommend whether or not the accused person should be hospitalized under compulsion.

The political role of psychiatrists examining persons accused of political "crimes" could not be clearer. Soviet psychiatrists will continue to exercise a political role as long as the expression of officially unapproved-of political opinions remains a crime in Soviet law.

A number of official psychiatric diagnoses on the basis of which politically-dissident Soviet citizens have been confined to psychiatric hospitals are available outside the USSR. Some non-Soviet psychiatrists have expressed the view that it is impossible adequately to assess these diagnoses. Such psychiatrists emphasize the complexity of psychiatric diagnosis and the need for examination not only of full documentation in each individual case but of the person who is the subject of the diagnosis. Certain merit can be seen in this attitude. However, Amnesty International believes that these official psychiatric diagnoses, taken together with numerous first-hand and eye-witness accounts, provide strong evidence that in many cases Soviet forensic psychiatrists have given precedence to political rather than medical criteria in diagnosing persons accused of political "crimes".

In 1969, Gennady Shimanov, an Orthodox Christian, was sent to the Kashchenko psychiatric hospital in Moscow for psychiatric examination. According to Shimanov's account, the examining psychiatrist, Dr German Shafran, made clear throughout his investigation that Mr Shimanov was being investigated on account of his religious views and at one point told him:

> "You see, Gennady Mikhailovich . . . Everything that you just told us confirms us in the view that illness lies at the root of your "conversion". Of course you yourself cannot understand this; but you must have confidence in us: we are specialists. If you had grown up in a religious family or had

38.   Here it is the currently operative RSFSR Criminal Code.

lived somewhere in the West, well, then we could have looked at your religiousness in another way . . . But you were brought up in a family of non-believers . . . You are an educated person. I am ready even to admit that you know more about philosophy and religion than I do . . . And suddenly . . . wham! . . . you're religious! . . . It's very odd indeed . . . and makes one wonder if some abnormal process were not already developing in you in your youth, which later on brought you to religion."[39]

One might ascribe this statement to the narrow-mindedness of the psychiatrist were it not for the KGB influence which predominated throughout the case. Allegedly it was the KGB which ordered that a psychiatric diagnosis be carried out on Gennady Shimanov, who had not been arrested or charged with any criminal offence. According to Mr Shimanov, Dr Shafran at one point told him in connection with his admission that he had regularly expressed his religious views to friends and neighbours:

"Perhaps you have not been going outside the framework of the law. But what significance does that have? In actual fact you do harm to the existing regime, all the same, by bringing back straying sheep to the Church. And you know yourself, Gena, that this regime is pretty strict . . . and will not put up with such activity. Here you are talking about laws. Don't you realize that the Committee of State Security [KGB] doesn't give a damn for laws! Looking at you, I am sorry for you, Gena. Because you will inevitably be crushed. And it will be cold comfort for you that you are not the only one. Don't think I am trying to frighten you. I'm not directly involved . . . You do understand me? But I know something of life. I myself worked for five years in Kolyma — as a medical expert. And I am sorry that you are preparing for yourself a martyr's crown. This time I think you will get out of here all right. But afterwards perhaps quite soon . . . much sooner than you think, you will turn up here again. And it will be for good and all — for compulsory treatment".

"But compulsory treatment can only be prescribed by a court," [Mr Shimanov replied].

"Well, what of that? They'll fix a closed hearing. And what will you be able to prove? Especially with such a diagnosis."[40]

There have been numerous other individual cases in which examining psychiatrists have made plain that political rather than medical factors were dominant in their evaluation of politically-dissident individuals. Vladimir Borisov, a Leningrad electrician, has twice been confined to psychiatric hospitals, first in 1964 in connection with charges of "anti-Soviet agitation and propaganda" and again in 1969 when he was charged with "anti-Soviet slander". When in late June 1969 Mr Borisov's wife complained that he had been confined to psychiatric hospital because of his opinions, a psychiatrist allegedly replied ". . . he is unlucky; he is down on our register. What may be a symptom of opinions in a normal person is a sign of illness in your husband".[41] Another psychiatrist allegedly told Mr Borisov

39. G.M. Shimanov, "Notes From the Red House", in *Abuse of Psychiatry for Political Repression in the Soviet Union*, page 213.
40. Ibid, page 202.
41. "Vladimir Yevgenyevich Borisov", in *Abuse of Psychiatry for Political Repression in the Soviet Union*, page 148.

"Listen Borisov, you're a normal fellow and I am sure you don't want to be sent to a madhouse. Why don't you change your views?"[42]

On 7 March 1974 the following conversation allegedly occurred during the examination of Evgeny Nikolayev, a scientist, by Dr V.D. Dmitrievsky in Moscow's Kashchenko ordinary psychiatric hospital:

*Dmitrievsky:* . . . I am interested in your own opinions. In the clinic which sent you to this hospital they made a point about your incorrect opinions about our society.

*Nikolayev:* Whatever my views may be they have nothing to do with psychiatry.

*Dmitrievsky:* If that were so you wouldn't be here. If your social views were not socially dangerous they would not have put you in a psychiatric hospital. The last three times you were in a psychiatric hospital was it for long periods?

*Nikolayev:* Yes, long.

*Dmietrievsky:* So you know our state machine. We are all subordinate to the appropriate organs, and if we get a directive from these organs we are obliged to fulfil it . . . You see, you're not well-known like Solzhenitsyn. For his statements and opinions they sent him out of the country. But they'll put you in a psychiatric hospital for your statements and opinions.[43]

In those psychiatric diagnoses of political dissidents which are available to us, a great deal of attention is invariably devoted to the political records of the subjects of psychiatric investigation. As Roy Medvedev stated in a submission to the Moscow Human Rights Committee in 1971:

In the conclusions of several psychiatric "special expert diagnoses" it is possible to find such "symptoms" of "psychiatric illness": "an obsessive mania for truth-seeking", "wears a beard", "meticulousness of thought and insufficiently critical attitude toward the existing situation", "considers the entry of Soviet troops into Czechoslovakia to have been aggression" . . . "thinks that he must devote his life to the ideal of communism".[44]

Zhores Medvedev (twin brother of Roy Medvedev) himself was temporarily committed to a psychiatric hospital under civil proceedings in 1970. Dr A.Ye. Lifshits, head doctor of the Kaluga Psychiatric Hospital and in charge of "diagnosing" Zhores Medvedev, took a particular interest in several of his critical writings. According to Zhores Medvedev:

On the evening of 8 June, Lifshits spent a long time trying to convince me that to engage in "publicist" writing in addition to one's normal professional work, scientific or other, was a sign of a "split" or "disassociated" personality, an obvious symptom of illness. "In time, of course, the hospital will discharge you", he said, "but you must completely stop all this other activity and concentrate on experimental work. If you continue your publicist activities, then you will inevitably end up back here with us."

42. Ibid.
43. *Samizdat* "A Conversation with a Psychiatrist", in *Khronika Zashchity Prav SSSR* (Khronika Press, New York) Number 12, pages 26-27.
44. R.A. Medvedev, "O Prinuditel'nykh Psikhiatricheskikh Gospitalizatsiyakh Po Politicheskom Motivam", in *Proceedings of the Moscow Human Rights Committee*, page 131.

Lifshits repeated this "prognosis" many times in different guises.[45]

Whatever the motivations of the psychiatrists involved, such judgements usually do not disguise acceptance of the security organs' viewpoint that political dissidence can reasonably be explained in terms of mental disturbance. Unapproved-of efforts to seek reform of Soviet institutions are frequently recorded as "reformist delusions", while an individual's refusal to recant often goes into the diagnosis as "absence of a critical attitude to his situation".

Diagnoses submitted by psychiatrists to the courts are frequently outlandish in their efforts to prove the presence of mental illness in political dissidents. For example, in 1972 a number of persons were arrested in Siberia for organization of a Buddhist sect. The most prominent of the group, Bidya Dandaron, was sentenced to a long term in a prison camp where he subsequently died.[46] His four co-defendants (Yu.K. Lavrov, A. Zheleznov, D. Butkus and V.M. Montlevich) were all submitted to psychiatric diagnosis, declared mentally ill and consigned by court order to psychiatric hospital.[47] A similar example of collective hospitalization occurred in 1971 when a psychiatric commission recommended that four persons from a group of seven Leningrad communists arrested for propagating dissident Marxism be confined to a special psychiatric hospital.[48]

The full texts of the official diagnoses made in these cases are not available to Amnesty International. However, it is difficult to believe that these cases of declaring insane whole groups of nonconforming persons were the result of some theory of group hysteria. Much more likely is that these official actions were dictated by political considerations.

It is clear that in a number of political cases Soviet psychiatrists have attempted to disguise politically-motivated decisions by the use of arcane terminology and concepts which are unintelligible to laymen. This device has been initiated from the highest level of Soviet psychiatry. It is essential to the abuse of psychiatry for political purposes because it enables psychiatrists to shield their purportedly expert conclusions from the judgement of ordinary citizens. The viewpoint that only a select group of experts can judge upon the fitness of certain categories of persons was put succinctly by a number of the most prominent Soviet psychiatrists in a 1973 letter to Western newspapers:

> There is a small number of mental cases whose disease, as a result of a mental derangement, paranoia and other psycho-pathological symptoms, can lead them to anti-social actions which fall in the category of those that are prohibited by law, such as disturbance of public order, dissemination of slander, manifestation of aggressive intentions, etc. It is noteworthy that they can do this after preliminary preparations, with a "cunningly calculated plan of action", as the founder of Russian forensic psychiatry V.P. Serbsky, who was widely known for his progressive views, wrote. To the people around them such mental cases do not create the impression of being obviously "insane". Most often these are persons suffering from

45.  Zhores and Roy Medvedev, *A Question of Madness* (Penguin Books, London, 1974), page 133.
46.  *The Observer* (London), 1 December 1974. See above, pages 26-27.
47.  *A Chronicle of Current Events,* Number 28, page 25.
48.  *Ibid*, Number 26, pages 229-230.

schizophrenia or a paranoid pathological development of the personality. Such cases are known well both by Soviet and foreign psychiatrists.

The seeming normality of such sick persons when they commit socially dangerous actions is used by anti-Soviet propaganda for slanderous contentions that these persons are not suffering from a mental disorder.[49]

The consequences of the dismissal of "seeming normality" as a decisive criterion in psychiatric analysis is well illustrated by the case of Olga Iofe. Miss Iofe, born in 1950, became involved with distribution of *samizdat* in 1966 and was arrested in 1969 on charges of "anti-Soviet agitation and propaganda". She was submitted for psychiatric diagnosis by a commission at the Serbsky Institute, which declared that she was suffering from "creeping schizophrenia". When Miss Iofe's case was heard in court on 20 August 1970, the court rejected a defence petition to allow Miss Iofe herself to be present at the hearing, but allowed her parents to represent her. According to *A Chronicle of Current Events*, "all the witnesses" testified in court that in their opinion Miss Iofe was of sound mind and of good character. To Dr Martynenko, chairman of the psychiatric diagnosis commission, this was irrelevant, as is indicated by her answers to questions put to her by the defence counsel Yu. V. Pozdeyev:

*Question:* Exactly what physiological tests were carried out to establish that she was suffering from an illness?

*Answer:* Such physiological tests are carried out on everybody without exception. The absence of symptoms of an illness cannot prove the absence of the illness itself.

*Question:* On the basis of exactly what remarks did the commission establish that her thought-processes were functioning on different levels? Describe even one of the tests administered to Olga, by means of which major disturbances of her thought-processes were established, or give even one remark by her which suggested such disturbances.

*Answer:* I am unable to give a concrete answer, and if the court requires one it will be necessary to send to the Serbsky Institute for the history of the illness. However, her reaction to being taken to the Serbsky Institute may serve as an example of her behaviour. She knew where she had been taken and realized what this meant, but she showed no sign of emotion, the tone of her voice didn't even change.

*Question:* Do you not ascribe Olga's behaviour to her self-control, strength of will and serenity, of which the witnesses have spoken?

*Answer:* It's impossible to control oneself to that extent.

*Question:* How do you explain the fact that the presence of an illness, which, according to the diagnosis, has been developing in O. Iofe since she was 14, did not prevent her from successfully graduating from the mathematical school and entering the university?

*Answer:* The presence of this form of schizophrenia does not presuppose changes in the personality noticeable to others.[50]

49.   *The Guardian* (London), 29 October 1973. Among the 21 signatories were Georgy Morozov and Andrei Snezhnevsky, both active at the Serbsky Institute in Moscow.
50.   *A Chronicle of Current Events*, Number 15. The defence counsel Yu. V. Pozdeyev, who also defended a number of other political defendants, subsequently lost his

Despite the absence in Miss Iofe of obvious symptoms of mental illness and despite the absence of any indication that Miss Iofe's behaviour was physically dangerous, the psychiatric commission recommended that she be sent to a special psychiatric hospital: that is, an institution legally designated for persons who represent "a special danger for society".[51]

A similar phenomenon can be observed in the case of Ivan Yakhimovich. In June 1969, a psychiatric commission in Riga examined Mr Yakhimovich, a communist who had earned high official praise as a collective farm chairman until in 1968 "he began spreading slanderous and defamatory statements blaming the Soviet government and social system". The psychiatrists could discover nothing abnormal in Mr Yakhimovich's record of behaviour apart from his political activity. The commission's official diagnosis included the following:

> Patient is completely oriented . . . The patient has an excellent knowledge of literature, of classics of Marxism and Leninism, and also has an excellent knowledge of works of many philosophers and political figures . . . During the interview with the psychiatrists, patient was polite, gentle, and showed no evidence of delusions and hallucinations, and displayed adequate memory.[52]

The commission's conclusion and recommendations were something of a *non sequitur*:

> On the basis of the above findings, the committee reaches the conclusion that Yakhimovich shows development of a paranoid system in a psychopathic personality . . . The patient is in need of compulsory treatment in the hospital of special regime.[53]

Frequently, when local psychiatric commissions have not found political defendants to be mentally ill, second diagnoses have been sought. Very often it is the Serbsky Institute which has been brought in to provide this second diagnosis, for example in the cases of Pyotr Grigorenko, Anatoly Chinnov, Nataliya Gorbanyevskaya and Leonid Plyushch. In these cases and in others, the Serbsky Institute's psychiatrists have overturned the findings of local psychiatrists that the defendants were not mentally ill. In at least several such cases, the Serbsky Institute has employed psychiatric criteria so subtle that not only laymen including the defendants themselves but even other psychiatrists have been unable to use them in evaluating the behaviour of these defendants.

The psychiatric diagnoses of General Pyotr Grigorenko, a prominent dissident Marxist-Leninist, exemplify this phenomenon. In 1969, after a Tashkent psychiatric commission had examined General Grigorenko and declared him to be mentally healthy, the Serbsky Institute of Forensic Psychiatry in Moscow was asked for a second opinion. This second diagnosis found in General Grigorenko's political activity clear signs of "pathological (paranoid) development of the personality". In recommending that General Grigorenko be confined to a "special" (i.e. maximum security) psychiatric hospital, the Serbsky Institute's experts noted the

clearance (*dopusk*) to defend in political trials. See Valery Chalidze, *To Defend These Rights: Human Rights and the Soviet Union,* page 130.
51.    RSFSR Criminal Code, Article 59.
52.    "Official Psychiatric Diagnoses — I.A. Yakhimovich: Report Number 96", in *Abuse of Psychiatry for Political Repression in the Soviet Union,* pages 170-171.
53.    Ibid, page 172.

deficiencies in the way the Tashkent commission had come to its opposite conclusion:

> The commission cannot agree with the outpatient forensic psychiatric diagnosis formulated in Tashkent since it has noted the presence in Grigorenko of pathological changes in his psyche recorded in the present report which could not be revealed in the conditions of an out-patient examination because of his outwardly well-adjusted behaviour, his formally coherent utterances and his retention of his past knowledge and manners — all of which is characteristic of a pathological development of the personality.[54]

In their *samizdat* "Handbook on Psychiatry for Dissidents", prepared in a Perm corrective labour colony in 1974, Semyon Gluzman and Vladimir Bukovsky discussed the absence of any clear demarcation between "normal" articulation of opinions and manifestations of "creeping schizophrenia" and "pathological development of the personality" as formulated by Soviet psychiatrists in the Serbsky Institute:

> ... the demonstrability of this sort of illness ["creeping schizophrenia" and "pathological development of the personality"] is very limited. Conversly, try to prove that your opinion about the occupation of Czechoslovakia or about the absence of democratic freedoms in the USSR is not a mistaken opinion but on the contrary has a real basis. Or that the shadowing of you and your near ones is not "persecution mania". Or that your subjective evaluation of domestic political life in the USSR is not immaterial when related to actual facts. Or that your "release" from your job after you added your signature to a "statement of protest" is an infringement of your rights.[55]

In sum, where political factors are involved in a case, the officially designated forensic psychiatry commissions clearly appear not to meet a reasonable standard of objectivity and scientific authority. It would obviously be of benefit to purportedly mentally ill persons if they could appeal to a second psychiatric commission working independently of the officially-designated psychiatrists. This is, however, completely excluded in Soviet practice.

In 1971, a Kiev psychiatrist Semyon Gluzman, together with two anonymous colleagues, wrote an "alternative" diagnosis on Pyotr Grigorenko.[56] In this diagnosis, Dr Gluzman *et al* evaluated much biographical detail and other information concerning General Grigorenko which was not mentioned in the Serbsky Institute's official diagnosis cited above. They concluded that General Grigorenko had pursued goals which were perhaps punishable by law, but that his condition could not be considered "a psychotic one of non-accountability".

In May 1972, Dr Gluzman was arrested and charged with "anti-Soviet slander". In October 1972 he was sentenced in Kiev to 7 years in a strict regime corrective

54. "Report Number 59/5: 'An In-Patient Forensic Diagnosis of P.G. Grigorenko', in *Abuse of Psychiatry for Political Repression in the Soviet Union*, page 70.
55. Semyon Gluzman and Vladimir Bukovsky, "Handbook on Psychiatry for Dissenters". This *samizdat* document arrived outside the USSR in February 1975. It has been reproduced in English in *Survey* (London), Numbers 94-95, Winter-Spring 1975.
56. This document was published in Russian in *Russkaya Mysl'* (Paris), 12 April 1973; in French in *Cahiers du Samizdat* (Brussels), May 1973; and in English by Radio Liberty.

labour colony, to be followed by 3 years in exile. The presiding magistrate was Judge Dyshel, who also presided in Leonid Plyuschch's case some months later.

The degree to which Soviet forensic psychiatry has been compromised in relation to political dissent is reflected in Gluzman's and Bukovsky's "Handbook on Psychiatry for Dissidents". This "handbook" advises persons threatened with compulsory detention in a psychiatric hospital how best to convince examining psychiatrists of their sanity:

> It is fatal to emphasize the moral qualities of the dissidents: truthfulness, honour and sympathy, because that would mean to give truthful responses which harm oneself and provide the psychiatrist with the symptoms he needs.[57]

Mr Bukovsky and Dr Gluzman recommend that the political dissident tell the psychiatrists that his political activities were due to ignorance of the possible consequences and by desire for fame. If he is nonetheless ordered confined to a psychiatric hospital, he must use "every possible tactical trick" to convince the psychiatrists that he has changed his political views.[58]

The report of a forensic psychiatric commission does not have the strength of law, but must be submitted together with other evidence to a court hearing of the case. In an earlier section of this report, it was stated that every political case brought before a Soviet court brings a "guilty" verdict. Political defendants diagnosed as mentally ill have fared no better in court. In no known such case has a Soviet court decided in favour of the defendant on the grounds that his constitutional or procedural rights had been violated. Such grounds have been available in many political cases, despite the general lack of fixed procedural rights for purportedly mentally ill persons. The Ukrainian cyberneticist Leonid Plyushch, for example, was held in pre-trial detention for one year, in direct violation of Article 34 of the USSR Fundamentals of Criminal Procedure.[59] During the whole of this period, and for six months thereafter, he was not allowed to meet with his wife.[60] These violations were not mentioned at the court hearing of Mr Plyushch's case.

Furthermore, the courts themselves have sometimes added their own procedural violations to those committed by the investigation officials. Again in Mr Plyushch's case, Judge Dyshel classified as a state secret the court hearing on Mr Plyushch's state of mind and ordered that the hearing be held *in camera*, in spite of Ukrainian legislation requiring that such hearings be open to the public.[61]

Judge Dyshel also refused to allow court witnesses to give evidence in favour of the defendant. Finally, the judge did not allow Mr Plyushch's legal representative (his wife) to participate in the hearing.[62] Consequently:

> The courtroom was empty: neither the accused, nor his legal representative, nor a psychiatric expert, nor the accused's relatives were present.

57. Gluzman and Bukovsky, "Handbook on Psychiatry for Dissidents" (1974).
58. Ibid.
59. T.S. Khodorovich (editor), *Istoriya Boleznyi Leonida Plyushcha*, (Herzen Foundation: Amsterdam, 1974), page 168.
60. Ibid, page 99.
61. Ibid, page 87.
62. Ibid, page 174.

So great was the isolation of the hearing from the outside world that the militia detachment guarding the empty hall refused (with threats of arrest) to allow onto the steps of the court building the citizens wishing to attend the hearing. It was only after many requests that the accused's wife and sister were allowed (on account of the severe cold) to await the end of hearing in the vestibule.[63]

The most important criticism that can be made of court hearings of such cases is their uncritical attitude toward the psychiatric diagnoses submitted. The psychiatric diagnoses which we have cited above, and others, are at the very least questionable as recommendations for court action. One course of action which is available to courts presented with unclear or incomplete diagnoses is to call for a second psychiatric opinion.[64] This is almost never done. Instead, Soviet courts in political cases almost invariably accept not only the findings of forensic psychiatric commissions, but their recommendations as to what should be done with the accused. If, as normally happens, the court accepts the psychiatric commission's diagnosis and recommendations, it then releases the defendant from criminal responsibility or punishment and orders measures conducive to the individual's medical recovery and at the same time protective of society.

One option open to the court does not entail detention of the defendant. The court may transfer him to the care of his relatives or guardians, at the same time ordering obligatory medical supervision.[65] However, such a decision may be made only if the court decides that the accused does not require compulsory medical treatment.

If the court, advised by a forensic psychiatric commission, decides that the accused requires compulsory medical treatment, it orders that he be confined either to an ordinary or a special psychiatric hospital for an indefinite period. According to the RSFSR Criminal Code, ordinary psychiatric hospitals are intended for persons who have committed not especially serious actions, while the special institutions are designed for persons who "represent a special danger to society".[66] A 1966 official textbook on Soviet criminal law, as its example of a person sent by court to an ordinary psychiatric hospital, cited a certain "B", a Leningrad woman:

> who during an argument with her neighbour slashed her in the face with a large table knife and, after dislodging several teeth, inflicted less serious wounds to her body.[67]

The political dissidents on whom documentation is available have no records of violence nor have the psychiatric commissions examining them even attempted to show that they represent a violent threat to others. Yet in deciding such cases, Soviet courts have almost invariably ordered the most severe forms of compulsory detention: confinement to special psychiatric hospitals for an indefinite period.

63.  Ibid, page 177.
64.  RSFSR Code of Criminal Procedure, Article 81.
65.  RSFSR Criminal Code, Article 60.
66.  Ibid., Article 59.
67.  *Ugolovnoye Pravo: Chast' Obshchaya* (Moscow, 1966), page 448.

122

## Special Psychiatric Hospitals

The court's decision as to whether a person should be sent to an ordinary or a special psychiatric hospital is of great importance to the individual's conditions of existence. Physical conditions and regulations in ordinary psychiatric hospitals are by all accounts much less severe than those prevailing in special psychiatric hospitals.[68] Since persons accused of political "offences" and declared mentally ill have as a rule been sent to special psychiatric hospitals, most of the available documentation of conditions in Soviet psychiatric hospitals concerns the "special" institutions, rather than "ordinary" ones. For both these reasons, this report will focus on conditions in special psychiatric hospitals.

There are seven major special psychiatric hospitals in the USSR. They are usually referred to by the names of the city in which they are located:

> Kazan (in the Tatar ASSR)
> Sychyovka (in Smolensk region)
> Leningrad (on Arsenalnaya Street, and hence often referred to as the "Arsenalnaya")
> Chernaykhovsk (in Kaliningrad region, formerly part of East Prussia)
> Minsk (in Belorossiya)
> Dnepropetrovsk (in the city of that name in the Ukraine)
> Oryol (in Oryol region)

In addition, in early 1972 two new special psychiatric hospitals were opened in Blagoveshchensk (in Amur province in the Soviet Far East) and in Kzyl-Orda (in Kazakhstan).[69] It should be noted that while considerable documentation is available on six of these institutions, there is little information available on those in Minsk and Kzyl-Orda and almost nothing on Blagoveshchensk.

Female patients consigned to a special psychiatric hospital invariably go to the Kazan institution. The institution in Sychyovka contains a "psychiatric colony" for extremely violent and incurably ill psychiatric patients. Of all institutions of detention in the USSR, the Sychyovka special psychiatric hospital is the most notorious.

Although it is officially recognized in the USSR that compulsory confinement in a psychiatric hospital is a form of detention, there is no legal code governing conditions of detention in such hospitals as there are for corrective labour institutions. Commentaries on the passages in the criminal and civil legislation which deal with this form of detention almost entirely ignore the problem of conditions and functioning of psychiatric hospitals. Conditions in psychiatric hospitals are specified only in ministerial regulations.

The only published "instruction" on the operations of psychiatric hospitals and the only one cited by official Soviet sources dates from 14 February 1967. It is entitled "Instruction on the System of Application of Compulsory Treatment and Other Measures of Medical Character in relation to Mentally Ill Persons Who Have Committed Socially Dangerous Acts".[70] This document contains only 30 brief articles, and a large proportion of its contents are devoted to repetition

68. A. Yesenin-Volpin, "Mneniye Eksperta Komiteta Prav Cheloveka", in *Proceedings of the Moscow Human Rights Committee,* pages 144-146.
69. *A Chronicle of Current Events,* Number 24, page 146.
70. Text in *Byulliten Verkhovnogo Suda SSSR,* Number 4, 1967, pages 37-39.

*Above:* Front view of the Arsenalnaya special psychiatric hospital in Leningrad.

*Above:* The Oryol special psychiatric hospital.

of general clauses in the criminal and civil procedural codes. As for the actual operation of psychiatric hospitals, the 1967 instruction confines itself almost exclusively to the system of documentation of inmates' cases and to their pension rights. This instruction in no way regulates conditions of detention. If the corrective labour codes are subject to criticism for failing to lay down sufficiently detailed regulations, there are no detailed regulations at all for psychiatric hospitals, or at least none which are available in print to the public.

This situation reflects and perpetuates the most important and disadvantageous peculiarity in the position of inmates of psychiatric hospitals: withdrawal of their status as rational subjects of the law. This status is specifically granted to inmates of corrective labour institutions: they formally retain the rights of Soviet citizens, with limitations, and they have the formal right to protest at violations of the law perpetrated against them. Persons committed to psychiatric hospitals are apparently not formally denied their status as citizens possessed of the right to claim legal redress against illegalities committed against them. However, the omission in law of specific guarantees of retention of this status opens the way for its deprivation. The impulse to reduce psychiatric inmates to the status of wards comes both from their passive condition as patients purportedly needing to be cured and from the prejudice (not unique to the USSR) that the mentally ill are not capable of recognizing their own interests.

A most important consequence of this is that inmates of Soviet special psychiatric hospitals have no guaranteed process by which to seek redress of psychiatric and juridical errors or abuses. They may write letters only at the discretion of their doctors, and then usually only to relatives. Inmates are normally not allowed to keep writing materials except at specific times allowed them for writing letters. Doctors can, in the course of prescribing treatment, forbid an inmate to read or write. This was ordered for Victor Fainberg[71] and for Pyotr Grigorenko.[72] When General Grigorenko protested about this to a regular psychiatric commission, he was allegedly told:

> "What do you need a pen for? You'll start getting ideas and writing them down, which is not permitted in your case."[73]

In their outward correspondence, prisoners may not describe their medical treatment or conditions of confinement. Efforts to do so are liable to be recorded as evidence of continued mental illness. For example, an official psychiatric diagnosis of Vladimir Borisov noted in relation to his state of mind:

> In the hospital he more than once tried to have letters of unpermitted content conveyed outside through patients and visitors.[74]

Inmates in special psychiatric hospitals have no contact with legal authorities. Although as far as Amnesty International knows it is not legally forbidden for them to consult a lawyer, it is extremely rare for an inmate to have any contact with a lawyer during his period of detention. Nor are they allowed to write to the procu-

71. *A Chronicle of Current Events,* Number 19, page 179.
72. *Samizdat* essay by Alexander Yesenin-Volpin, "Let Pyotr Grigorenko Have a Fountain Pen" (1970).
73. *A Chronicle of Current Events,* Number 18, page 105.
74. "Official Psychiatric Diagnosis: Report Number 575 (Outpatient)", in *Abuse of Psychiatry for Political Repression in the Soviet Union,* page 151.

racy, although the procuracy is legally charged with supervision of psychiatric institutions.[75]

For the duration of their confinement in a special psychiatric hospital, inmates are almost totally cut off from the outside world, and are "at the disposal" of the authorities who administer those institutions and the psychiatrists who staff them.

Special psychiatric hospitals are in the direct administration of the MVD (Ministry of Internal Affairs) rather than of the health organs.[76] To appreciate this fact it is necessary to recollect the nature of the MVD. The MVD shares with the KGB (State Security Committee) the heritage of the NKVD (People's Commissariat of Internal Affairs), the organ which directly administered political control during much of the Stalin period. While many of the NKVD's more overtly political functions are now exercised by the KGB, the MVD retains vast powers. It administers most of the country's police forces, and has large armed forces of its own which are quite separate from the regular armed forces. The MVD is entrusted by law to investigate cases falling under a number of articles of the criminal codes. In addition to administering penal institutions, the MVD also exercises supervision and surveillance of released prisoners, a function which works to the particular disadvantage of former political prisoners. The MVD has retained a strongly political role, one manifestation of which is the hostility of MVD officers to political prisoners as already indicated in this report.

While it might be argued that regular prison institutions fall logically within the competence of internal security organs, this cannot be said of hospital institutions which are supposedly intended to provide medical treatment. The fact that special psychiatric hospitals are administered directly by the MVD indicates that, at the least, security factors are given priority over medical considerations in the administration of such institutions. However, the conclusion is unavoidable that the MVD's direct control of these institutions infuses the functioning of special psychiatric hospitals with a political element which may be irrelevant for some inmates, but which is decisive for the fate of those who have engaged in criticism of established institutions such as the MVD itself.

Many special psychiatric hospitals are located in buildings formerly used as prisons. For example, the building of the Leningrad special psychiatric hospital on Arsenalnaya street was a women's prison before the 1917 revolution and up to 1949; the Oryol special psychiatric hospital occupies part of a famous Tsarist prison known as the "Orlovskyi Tsentral"; the Chernyakhovsk special psychiatric hospital (in Kaliningrad — formerly Könisberg — region) is situated in a former German prison; the Sychyovka psychiatric colony (in Smolensk region) is located in prison buildings dating back to the 18th century. The Dnepropetrovsk special psychiatric hospital (in the Ukraine) is also housed in a former prison.

In law, compulsory detention for psychiatric treatment is not a form of punishment.[77] Special psychiatric institutions are called "hospitals",[78] and their in-

75. Edict on Procuracy Supervision in the USSR (1955), Article 22.
76. *Sovetskoye Ugolovnoye Pravo: Chast' Obshchaya* (Moscow: 1972), page 463.
77. *Commentary to the RSFSR Criminal Code* (1971), page 149.
78. Until the mid-1950s, they were officially classified as prison institutions. See Alexander Yesenin-Volpin, "Mneniye Eksperta Komiteta Prav Cheloveka A.S. Volpina", in *Proceedings of the Moscow Human Rights Committee*, page 142.

mates "patients". However, such institutions resemble prisons in the intensity of security measures. These hospitals are surrounded by formidable exterior walls and, within these walls, by barbed wire.[79] Armed military personnel and dogs guard them. Hospital personnel, including hospital directors, heads of departments and many of the psychiatrists, are officers in the MVD.

The regimen to which inmates are subjected resembles that in penal institutions. Many inmates are kept in cells. The principle difference lies in the absence of laws governing conditions in psychiatric hospitals, which are regulated by MVD instructions. There is not even a formal requirement that instructions be posted where patients can see them.

Inmates are allowed a daily exercise period (a walk) of only one hour. Lights burn all night in cells and wards. Patients may not possess cash or whatever objects the administrators and psychiatrists may forbid.

Like inmates of prisons, patients in special psychiatric hospitals are subject to rigorous discipline. The absence of a legal code of regulations, however, greatly expands the possibility for requiring patients to obey arbitrary orders. According to the mathematician and poet Alexander Yesenin-Volpin:

> It is assumed that the patient must submit to the orders of anybody . . .
> even to the demands of orderlies who are convicts. If he does not do this,
> the doctor can draw unfavourable conclusions about his psychiatric con-
> dition.[80]

What renders this working policy particularly dangerous and inhumane is the heinous practice of recruiting convicted criminals prisoners from the corrective labour institutions to serve as orderlies (*sanitary*) in the special psychiatric hospitals. According to an anonymous "witness" who spent time in the Sychyovka corrective labour colony, at any given time 200 prisoners from that colony worked as orderlies in the adjacent psychiatric hospital.[81] Other accounts indicate that this practice is common to other special psychiatric hospitals in the USSR.

According to Victor Fainberg (who, after taking part in a demonstration in Red Square against the occupation of Czechoslovakia by Warsaw Pact troops, spent several years in the Leningrad special psychiatric hospital) this practice is officially justified as part of the "re-education" of such convicts.[82] In fact, these convicts receive no training suitable for work in hospitals, and are more likely to be corrupted than reformed by the conditions under which they do this work.

These convict-orderlies are given considerable authority to ensure that prisoners maintain discipline. It is widely reported that the contempt which many of them feel for the patients, is such that they call them "fools" (*duraki*) even in their presence.[83] The following statement by an eye-witness of conditions in the Sychyovka psychiatric colony speaks for itself:

> The patients cannot carry out their natural bodily functions, since the or-
> derlies do not always on the first request take them to the toilets. The

79.     Ibid.
80.     Ibid, page 143.
81.     "A Witness' Story: The Special Psychiatric Hospital in the City of Sychyovka in
        Smolensk Region (P/Ya Ya/O 100/6)", in *Istoriya Boleznyi Leonida Plyushcha*, page 9
82.     Victor Fainberg, "Appeal to Human Rights Organizations" (July 1970), in *Abuse of
        Psychiatry for Political Repression in the Soviet Union*, page 141.
83.     *Istoriya Boleznyi Leonida Plyushcha*, page 95.

patients themselves do not have the right to go by themselves, and therefore they sometimes have to wait for several hours.[84]

With the approval of regular hospital staff, convict-orderlies on a regular basis beat prisoners in what can only be described as a sadistic manner.

In a 1970 interview with the Associated Press journalist Holger Jenson, Vladimir Bukovsky told about treatment meted out by the convict-orderlies to some of his fellow inmates in the Leningrad special psychiatric hospital in 1964:

They beat the Ukrainian every day, just tied him up and kicked him in the stomach. Sometimes they would put inmates in padded isolation cells and beat them almost continuously. I know of several men who died after this, and the clinic above us was always full.[85]

A former inmate of the Sychovka corrective labour colony recollected several conversations with a criminal prisoner who served as an orderly in the neighbouring psychiatric colony. One prisoner, a formerly orderly, remembered nostalgically:

"It's good to work in the nuthouse: there's always something to eat and someone to hit in the mouth."

"But why hit people?"

"Here's why. You're standing in the middle of a corridor. A fool comes along, slinking against the wall. You're bored, you see. You just give him one in the mouth, and it cheers you up."

Another orderly, a tall, husky, healthy fellow complained:

"My hands hurt today."

"Why do they hurt?"

"I cudgelled one fool."[86]

Victor Fainberg, in a 1970 "Appeal to Human Rights Organizations", provided details of numerous instances of brutal beating of patients in the Leningrad special psychiatric hospital (where Mr Fainberg was at the time confined) and the names of those allegedly involved. The role of regular hospital staff in these events is particularly shocking.

What is known as "discipline" is maintained by a deliberately created atmosphere of intimidation. Cases of orderlies, warders and block superintendents beating up patients are frequent. Beating is considered a normal phenomenon here. As a rule it takes place with the silent approval of the nurses and obvious connivance of the doctors. Here's an example of a doctor's instruction to orderlies:

"Don't you know you're not supposed to beat people, especially if you don't know how to do it?"

When a patient, Semenchuk, was beaten up by orderlies and a duty warder on the staircase and then in his cell, the duty doctor, Tatyana Alekseyevna, made the following wise comment on the beating to the patient:

"Come on, stand up, you won't break your head!"[87]

84. Ibid, page 96.
85. Holger Jensen, "The Experiences of Vladimir Bukovsky" (Associated Press news agency dispatch from Moscow, 13 May 1970).
86. "A Witness' Story: The Special Psychiatric Hospital in the city of Sychyovka in Smolensk Region (P/Ya Ya/O 100/6)" in *Istoriya Boleznyi Leonida Plyushcha*, page 95.
87. Victor Fainberg, "Appeal to Human Rights Organizations", *Abuse of Psychiatry for Political Repression in the Soviet Union*, pages 139-140.

Although such happenings are clearly illegal, inmates of psychiatric hospitals have no legal opportunity to seek redress. As was mentioned above, letters of complaint are not passed on to legal authorities, and any other form of complaint can go only as far as the hospital staff. Some political "patients" have used alternative methods of self-defence, such as hunger strikes and threats of suicide. These are likely to be successful only if strong interest in the case is shown from outside. For the great majority of patients, "sane" or "insane", there is no means of self-help against even the most brutal and degrading treatment.

For the duration of a patient's stay in a Soviet psychiatric hospital, his fate is technically in the hands of psychiatrists, doctors and administrators who staff the institution. The only justification for this situation is the inmate's need for medical treatment and the medical personnel's ability to assume the responsibility of deciding without the patient's consent what treatment is best for him.

However, as we have indicated above, medical practice in psychiatric hospitals is fundamentally affected by measures taken for the sake of greater security. Even if orderlies did not physically mistreat and neglect patients, it could hardly be argued that a system of discipline executed by convicted criminals was compatible with the kind of refined psychiatric treatment needed by genuinely ill patients. This is the more true in relation to political "patients", whose "mental illness" is usually so subtle in manifestation that only select psychiatrists can diagnose it.

The emphasis on the exigencies of security impinges directly on the medical work of psychiatrists in such institutions. Victor Fainberg stated in a letter smuggled out of the Leningrad special psychiatric hospital in 1970:

> In a special hospital there is a system of double subordination or double control, which results in two lines of supervision: (1) the chief physician, the head of the section, the doctor directly in charge, the nurse; and (2) the hospital duty officer, the block superintendent and the warder; they are all supposed to control one another. At the bottom of the two lines of subordination is the orderly, who is subordinate to both of them, but immediate control over him is exercised by the warder, i.e. by a person who has no connection whatsoever with medicine. Such a system not only fails to prevent arbitrariness but, as the result of the system of mutual "covering up" of one another's misdemeanours and of other well-established hospital traditions, actually encourages it. There are cases of orderlies being instructed by the warder to force their way into a ward and tie up and assault a patient without the knowledge of the nurse. The system at present is such that even people who feel some human sympathy for the patients are in practice unable to help them. Thus, a doctor who really wishes to protect a patient from the mockery and blows of the warders and block superintendents is not in a position to do this. A nurse can only ask a warder to refrain from rudeness and physical violence.[88]

The very fact that many of the psychiatrists are officers in the MVD indicates that in their work they are at least partly guided by considerations extraneous to professional skills and ethics. In at least one case, the head of a special psychiatric hospital seems to have been appointed on the basis of qualifications having

---

88.    Victor Fainberg, "Appeal to Human Rights Organizations", *Abuse of Psychiatry for Political Repression in the Soviet Union,* page 142.

little relationship to psychiatry. It was reported in 1970 that Lieutenant-Colonel Baryshnikov, who at the time was director of the Oryol special psychiatric hospital, had previously been head of a sanitorium for tuberculosis patients. He had been trained as a surgeon, not as a psychiatrist. In the same institution, other doctors who were prescribing psychiatric treatment included an oculist, an ear, nose and throat specialist, and a general physician.[89]

Neither the patient nor his relatives has any influence in the selection of the psychiatrist assigned to his case. Psychiatrists are not obliged to tell their full names to patients' relatives.[90] Neither the patient nor his relatives may question the psychiatrist's decisions as to the type of medical treatment given to the patient, nor see the documentation on which these decisions are based.

This situation is yet another manifestation of institutionalized contempt for the rights of mental patients. The acknowledgement that some or even many psychiatric patients are not capable of rational assessment of medical decisions does not alter the fact that the total withdrawal from patients of any influence in determination of their medical treatment is conducive to arbitrary decisions on the part of doctors and psychiatrists. In special psychiatric hospitals, where patients are kept in almost total isolation from society and where non-medical criteria influence the appointment of psychiatrists, the anonymity of psychiatrists and the unchallengeable character of their decisions invite medical practices which are positively dangerous for patients.

One questionable practice is the widespread use of the drug sulphazin for non-medical purposes. This drug has been used in many countries "in certain difficult cases of schizophrenia and progressive paralysis".[91] It and similar treatments have in recent years been abandoned by psychiatric practice in many countries because "so few patients appeared to benefit"[92] and because of the extreme physical discomfort induced by it. Sulphazin induces a raging fever and causes stomach cramps, fever and intense pain.

Yet in Soviet special psychiatric hospitals, sulphazin is administered not only for medical purposes but as a form of punishment. Victor Fainberg remarked in 1970:

> . . . injections of sulphanilomide [apparently here Mr Fainberg was alluding to to sulphazin] are used almost exclusively as a punishment; the patient's temperature then rises to 40°C and for three days it is painful for him even to stir (not surprising when they give him a fifth injection two days later).[93]

The same practice was reported by Vladimir Bukovsky[94] and by Alexander Yesenin-Volpin.[95]

89. "Vladimir Gershuni writes from the special psychiatric hospital in Oryol", in *Abuse of Psychiatry for Political Repression in the Soviet Union,* page 230.
90. See for example *Istoriya Boleznyi Leonida Plyushcha,* pages 102, 105.
91. *Abuse of Psychiatry for Political Repression in the Soviet Union,* page 241.
92. Unpublished, paper by Dr. W.L. Tonge, "The Use of Mental Hospitals in the Control of Political Dissent" (London), page 29.
93. Victor Fainberg "Appeal to Human Rights Organizations", in *Abuse of Psychiatry for Political Repression in the Soviet Union,* page 141.
94. Holger Jenson, "The Experiences of Vladimir Bukosvky".
95. Alexander Yesenin-Volpin, "Mneniye Eksperta Komiteta Prav Cheloveka", page 139.

130

Another out-dated psychiatric device still in use in Soviet special psychiatric hospitals is the "wet-pack". This crude method of physically restraining violent patients was dropped from practice in many countries many years ago. Many eye-witnesses report that the wet-pack, like sulphazin, is used not only in respons to the patient's condition but as a form of punishment. According to Vladimir Bukovsky in a 1970 interview with William Cole, a correspondent of the Columbia Broadcasting System:

> The third form of punishment we used to call the "roll-up" — it involved th use of wet canvas — long pieces of it — in which the patient is rolled up fron head to foot, and so tightly that it was difficult for him to breathe, and as the canvas began to dry out it would get tighter and tighter and make the patient feel even worse. But that punishment was applied with some cautio — there were medical men present while it was taking place who made sure that the patient did not lose consciousness, and if his pulse began to weake then the canvas would be eased.[96]

Victor Fainberg witnessed the same practice in the Leningrad special psychiatric hospital:

> For the same purposes they use the so-called "roll-up" or "warm-moist roll", when the patient is tied up in damp sheets and not only fastened down to his bunk but cocooned as tightly as possible with strips of the sheets placed almost touching one another. The sheets dry out and squeeze the entire body as in a vice (the patient often loses consciousness), and the whole section can hear the wails of the tortured victim. There have bee cases when patients have been "rolled-up" on 10 successive days![97]

A recognized form of treating schizophrenia and certain other psychiatric disorders involves the administration of depressant drugs, including haloperidol, aminazin and triftazin. Even administered in carefully-regulated doses and with close consideration of the patient's condition, such drugs have extremely unpleasant side-effects: "toxic inflammation of the liver, elevation of intraocular pressure, fluctuations of arterial pressure, increased tension and cramping of the muscles, headaches, malaise, depressive moods, dryness of the mouth".[98]

These side-effects must be countered by administration of other counteracting medications. The application of these drugs to persons not suffering from the disorders for treatment of which they are suited causes "much unnecessary distress on account of the side effects".[99]

It is clear from the reports of involved parties that many psychiatrists in Soviet special psychiatric hospitals apply these drugs indiscriminately and with little regard for inmates' medical needs. Vladimir Gershuni, a Moscow worker diagnosed as mentally ill in 1969 in connection with his dissident activities, wrot from the Oryol institution in 1970:

> When our party of prisoners arrived from Butyrka, all 60 of us were prescribed treatment, without undergoing any medical examination. For in-

96. "Three Voices of Dissent", *Survey*, Number 77, (Autumn 1970), page 142.
97. Victor Fainberg, "Appeal to Human Rights Organizations", in *Abuse of Psychiatry for Political Repression jn the Soviet Union*, page 141.
98. *Abuse of Psychiatry for Political Repression in the Soviet Union*, page 241.
99. Unpublished paper by Dr W.L. Tonge "The Use of Mental Hospitals in the Control of Political Dissent" (London), page 29.

stance, they took my blood pressure, but the others were not given even that much attention. Almost all of those who arrived were given aminazin, both orally and by injection. No one showed any interest in either a patient's heart or his liver or anything that was wrong with him, if these had no bearing on psychiatry.[100]

Mr Gershuni described the effects of aminazin, and the steps taken by the medical staff when he complained:

March 11, morning: During rounds, just by way of an experiment, I complained about feeling poorly after taking haloperidol, and asked that the dose be reduced. This led to my being prescribed even more aminazin than I was already receiving. The head physician, Evgeni Vladimirovich Kozich, the oculist I have referred to already, being in charge of my case, made this decision. During a hunger strike in January (I had been given aminazin since my arrival), I felt steadily worse and worse, and after making a complaint, I began to get aminazin injections in the maximum dose, or very close to it (approximately 6 cc). I couldn't sleep at all, yet the same dose was administered to me for 12 days in a row, until they became convinced that I was still not sleeping, and that the injections had not made me give up my hunger strike. I was given two injections a day, from 7 to 18 January, and from 19 January onwards I have been given two tablets of haloperidol twice daily, that is four tablets in all (and Kozich assures me that this will go on for a long time). This medicine makes me feel more awful than anything I have experienced before; you no sooner lie down than you want to get up, you no sooner take a step than you're longing to sit down, and if you sit down, you want to walk again — and there's nowhere to walk. By the way, I'm not the only one who's had this sort of thing happen to him. Everyone here has their life made miserable by triftazin (Trifluoperazine/stelazine), aminazin, and other powerful drugs.[101]

Doctors in the Dnepropetrovsk special psychiatric hospital began on 22 August 1973 to treat Leonid Plyushch with haloperidol. As is clearly witnessed by letters to his family, Mr Plyushch had until that time retained a high standard of intellectual activity and was attempting to continue his study of the nature of mathematical and other forms of "games".[102] When on 22 October 1973 his wife, Tatyana Zhitnikova-Plyushch, visited him, she claims to have found him in the following condition after two months of treatment with haloperidol:

When they brought Leonid Ivanovich into the visiting room, it was impossible to recognize him. His eyes were full of pain and misery, he spoke with difficulty and brokenly, frequently leaning on the back of the chair in search of support. His effort at self-control was evident as from time to time he closed his eyes, trying to carry on a conversation and to answer questions. But his inner strength was exhausted, finished. Leonid Ivanovich began to gasp, to awkwardly unbutton his clothing . . .; his face was

100. "Vladimir Gershuni Writes from the Special Psychiatric Hospital in Oryol", in *Abuse of Psychiatry for Political Repression in the Soviet Union*, page 230. The identical phenomenon was observed by Valery Tarsis over a decade ago in his *Ward 7*.
101. Ibid, page 231.
102 Many of Leonid Plyushch's letters are reproduced in T. Khodorovich, *Istoriya Bolezynyi Leonida Plyushcha*, pages 11-86.

convulsed and he got cramp in his hands and legs . . . It was evident that from time to time he lost his hearing . . . Leonid Ivanovich could not control himself, and it was he who asked that the meeting be ended ten minutes ahead of time. They took him away.[103]

When after the visit Mrs Plyushch asked her husband's doctor (who refused to give her family name, identifying herself only as "Lidiya Alekseyevna") why he was being treated with haloperidol, the doctor allegedly replied: "Why do you have to know? We'll give him whatever is necessary."[104]

When Mrs Plyushch next visited her husband (6 November 1973), his state had further deteriorated. He told his wife that he was incapable of writing letters to her and that he did not want her to send him any more scientific books since he was incapable of reading them.[105] Mrs Plyushch again approached the psychiatrist charged with Mr Plyushch's case, asking why her husband had not at least been given medication to counteract the negative effects of haloperidol. The psychiatrist replied that she would divulge nothing, either about the diagnosis or about the treatment.[106]

In February and March 1974, doctors ceased administering haloperidol to Mr Plyushch and instead began to administer insulin, apparently in large doses.[107] At a meeting with his wife on 4 March 1974, Mr Plyushch was, by her account, unrecognizable:

Great dropsical swelling had occurred, he moved with difficulty, and his eyes had lost their liveliness.[108]

Possibly on account of Leonid Plyushch's serious physical condition, doctors have at least twice in 1974 temporarily ceased to treat him with drugs: in April and May, and in late June. Each time, his physical and mental condition improved.[109]

In November 1974, Mr Plyushch began to be injected with large doses of an anti-schizophrenic drug known as triftazin.[110] At the end of 1974, administration of drugs to Mr Plyushch was again temporarily halted, and when Mrs Plyushch visited him on 3 January 1975, his condition was improved. However, in a five line note later that month Mr Plyushch said that he was incapable of replying to her letters.[111]

On 20 December 1974, Mrs Plyushch wrote to the Dnepropetrovsk regional procurator requesting that criminal proceedings be initiated against the medical staff of the Dnepropetrovsk special psychiatric hospital. She asserted:

For the last one-and-a-half years my husband has been given incorrect medical treatment deliberately. This gives me the right to regard the actions of the hospital's medical personnel as criminal and to demand that they be examined in court.

103.  *Istoriya Boleznyi Leonida Plyushcha,* page 102.
104.  Ibid, page 103. It later became known that she is Dr L.A. Chasovskikh.
105.  Ibid, page 104.
106.  Ibid, page 105.
107.  *Khronika Tekushchikh Sobitii.* Number 32, page 53.
108.  Ibid.
109.  Ibid, pages 53-54.
110.  Information contained in *The New York Times* dispatch from Moscow, 19 December 1974. This information has been confirmed by other telephone calls to Moscow.
111.  Information received by telephone from Moscow in February 1975.

Soviet authorities have on a number of occasions claimed that psychiatrists and doctors who make wrong diagnoses or prescribe wrong treatments are subject to criminal responsibility. Mrs Plyushch's effort to initiate what amounts to a criminal malpractice suit against the medical staff of the Dnepropetrovsk special psychiatric hospital must be regarded as an important test of Soviet legal guarantees against abuses of psychiatry. Non-Soviet psychiatrists from a number of countries have written to the Dnepropetrovsk regional procurator expressing their interest in this matter and requesting permission to attend the court hearing. However, at the time this report was completed (September 1975) there was still no sign that Mrs Plyushch's request will be satisfied or that the matter will be discussed in court.

Many ex-inmates of Soviet special psychiatric hospitals assert cateogircally that the above-cited powerful drugs are deliberately administered to "patients" diagnosed "mentally ill" as a means of punishing them and, by destroying their intellectual capacity, as a means of removing their capability of holding "dissident" opinions.

Certainly in many cases "political patients" have suffered at least temporary intellectual incapacitation as a consequence of prolonged treatment with powerful drugs. This is reprehensible in itself, and even more blameworthy because of the manifest carelessness with which psychiatrists have submitted many "patients" to this "treatment". The degree of culpability incurred by the implicated Soviet psychiatrists depends on the answer to the question: why have such persons as Leonid Plyushch, Vladimir Borisov, Vladimir Gershuni and many others been treated with these drugs?

Some psychiatrists have answered this question by referring to variations in psychiatric opinion and attendant variations in the type of treatment which individual psychiatrists (in the USSR as elsewhere) are wont to prescribe. This answer is unsatisfactory. The "political patients" on whom substantial evidence is available to Amnesty International were diagnosed "mentally ill" on the most subtle of criteria, criteria comprehensible only to the psychiatrists responsible for the diagnoses.

Even if one accepted that these diagnoses were correct, it is scarcely conceivable that in such "borderline cases" responsible psychiatrists would, for the "patient's" benefit, regularly prescribe strong and continuing treatment with powerful drugs unaccompanied by other drugs of such a nature as to relieve the terrible suffering thus inflicted. In other words even if such persons as Plyushch, *et al* are mentally ill, they have been "treated" in an inhumane way which has subjected them to a degree and kind of suffering that their "illness" itself did not cause.

This abuse results from political considerations originating beyond the special psychiatric hospitals. Those who diagnose political "dissidents" as "mentally ill" may or may not believe them to be so. The point is that, objectively, the very goal of treating such patients in psychiatric hospitals is to obtain conformance with official norms, deviance from which was diagnosed as "mental illness". There is considerable evidence that the decision to use this method of obtaining conformance, or submission, is made not by psychiatrists but by state security officials. Much of this evidence has been cited above in reference to the process by

134

which persons are sent to psychiatric hospitals.

There is also considerable evidence that the specific form of psychiatric "treatment" given to political dissidents is decided outside the hospitals. The director (named Lyamin) of the Sychyovka special psychiatric hospital told the "patient" Yury Belov in 1972: "We aren't treating you for an illness but for your opinions."[112] In October 1973, the wife of Leonid Plyushch was summoned to meet an investigator of the Kiev City Procurator's office-named Kondratenko. Referring to her outspoken efforts on behalf of her husband, Mr Kondratenko allegedly told Mrs Plyushch:

"If you did not behave in this way, your husband's fate would be different."[113]

Many similar examples could be quoted.

## Release from Special Psychiatric Hospitals

Neither the law nor the decisions of courts ordering compulsory psychiatric treatment set any limit on the length of a person's confinement to a psychiatric hospital.

Compulsory treatment can be for an indefinite period if the illness turns out to be incurable.[114]

The criminal procedure codes stipulate that when the administration of the psychiatric institution, supported by the findings of a commission of doctors, recommends a person's release or transfer to a different type of psychiatric hospital, this proposal shall be considered by a court.[115] Ministerial instructions specify that each patient shall be examined by a psychiatric commission at six-monthly intervals.[116] This commission can recommend release, transfer to a different type of hospital or continued confinement for treatment in the same institution. Participation of a legal authority (i.e. someone from the procurator's office) is apparently optional in sessions of such commisssions[117] but does not appear to have occurred in any of the cases well known outside the USSR.

The bi-annual commissions have often been marred by abuses similar to those committed by the expert psychiatric commissions which initially recommend individuals' compulsory confinement for medical treatment. A gross example is provided by the March 1965 psychiatric commission which was called upon to recommend whether General Pyotr Grigorenko should be released from the Leningrad special psychiatric hospital. According to the unofficial diagnosis of General Grigorenko's case history by Semyon Gluzman *et al*, the chairman of the commission openly told General Grigorenko that the commission's decision had been pre-decided and had nothing to do with his mental health:

At a session of the expert commission dealing with his discharge, the chairman asked Grigorenko: "Pyotr Grigoriyevich, how do you want to be dis-

112.  *A Chronicle of Current Events,* Number 30, page 100.
113.  *Istoriya Boleznyi Leonida Plyushcha,* page 119.
114.  *Scientific — Practical Commentary to the RSFSR Code of Criminal Procedure* (1970), page 526.
115.  RSFSR Code of Criminal Procedure, Article 412.
116.  Instruction on the System of Application of Compulsory Treatment and Other Measures of a Medical Character to Mentally Ill Persons Who Have Committed Socially Dangerous Actions (February 1967), Article 23.
117.  Ibid.

charged? on the grounds of recovery, or shall we protest against the diagnoses? Only bear in mind that any consideration of the latter will take a long time." Grigorenko chose the former and was discharged on the grounds of his "full recovery". In the commission's report it was stated that he had admitted his actions to be mistaken.[118]

The last part of this statement bears out a charge invariably made by persons sent to psychiatric hospitals in connection with their political or religious activities: that such persons are liable to be released only if they recant their dissident views and in some way acknowledge that they have been mentally ill. The inmate's refusal to recant "anti-Soviet opinions" and his efforts to resist harmful forms of treatment or to protest at his confinement to the psychiatric hospital (are recorded as symptoms of persistence of a mental illness. In 1971, during General Grigorenko's second period of confinement in a special psychiatric hospital (this time in Kazan and lasting four years), a regular psychiatric commission allegedly asked him at the outset of their examination: "Pyotr Grigorevich, how are your convictions?" He replied that they were unchanged, and the commission ruled: "Treatment to be continued in view of the patient's unhealthy condition."[119]

In July 1974, Leonid Plyushch told his wife that he had been examined by a local commission of psychiatrists:

The members of the commission had put three questions to him: "How do you feel?" "All right." "How does the insulin affect you?" "It provokes an allergy." "How do you regard your former activity?" "I regret that I got involved in it." The commission decided to prolong his treatment.[120]

A doctor in the Leningrad special psychiatric hospital allegedly told Victor Fainberg in 1971:

"Your discharge depends on your conduct. By your conduct we mean your opinions precisely on political questions. Your disease is dissent. As soon as you renounce your opinions and adopt the correct point of view, we'll let you out."[121]

For Victor Fainberg, as for many other Soviet citizens in his situation, this demand was repugnant. He refused to submit and resorted instead to a series of hunger strikes and even suicide threats. It appears that these methods of self-defence together with strong outside interest in his case were decisive in securing Mr Fainberg's final release from compulsory confinement in 1974. Others have been even less fortunate. According to Vassily Chernishev's 1971 statement on his his own period of confinement to a psychiatric hospital, Nikolai Broslavsky had spent 25 years in such confinement because of refusal to compromise his religious convictions.[122] Other accounts by inmates of Soviet special psychiatric hospitals refer to many individuals thus confined for periods of time in excess of the maximum sentence for the crimes allegedly committed by them.

118. "Further Forensic Diagnosis in the case of Pyotr Grigoriyevich Grigorenko, born 1907, a Ukrainian citizen of Moscow, made (by Dr Semyon Gluzman and two other anonymous Soviet psychiatrists ) in the examinee's absence" (1971).
119. A Chronicle of Current Events, number 18, page 105.
120. Khronika Te kushchikh Sobitii, Number 32, page 54.
121. A Chronicle of Current Events, number 19, page 179.
122. "The Case of Vassily I. Chernishev", Abuse of Psychiatry for Political Repression in the Soviet Union, page 227.

If the psychiatric commission finds that a patient is sufficiently recovered to justify his release, this recommendation is brought before a court. Throughout a patient's stay in a psychiatric hospital, it is only on such an occasion that he has any contact with any institution outside the psychiatric hospital.

Yet even at this stage, non-medical factors can require that the now "medically-recovered" individual can be returned for compulsory psychiatric treatment. General Grigorenko claimed to know of cases where courts had rejected recommendations of release on the grounds that "the period of treatment does not correspond to the seriousness of the crime committed".[123] In November 1970, Victor Kuznetsov (a Moscow artist arrested in 1969 for possession of *samizdat*) was diagnosed as fit for release by an expert psychiatric commission in the Kazan special psychiatric hospital. When this recommendation reached the local court, the procurator (named Morozov) requested "in view of the gravity of Mr Kuznetsov's guilt" that his confinement in the hospital be prolonged. The court agreed with the procurator and Mr Kuznetsov was returned to the special psychiatric hospital.[124]

In April 1972, Victor Fainberg and Vladimir Borisov were taken from the Leningrad special psychiatric hospital to Moscow's Serbsky Institute where a diagnostic commission found them to be of sound mind.[125] A court hearing to decide upon their release was arranged for 10 July. However, the court, at the request of the procurator, refused to hear the case on the grounds that according to instructions, the Serbsky Institute's commission was not competent to recommend the release of Mr Fainberg and Mr Borisov, in spite of the fact that it was a Serbsky Institute commission that had originally diagnosed Mr Fainberg as mentally ill. The court ordered that Mr Fainberg be examined by the Central Forensic Psychiatric Diagnostic Commission, composed mainly of employees of the Serbsky Insttute.[126] When this examination was finally held in December 1972, the central commission recommended that Mr Fainberg be transferred to an ordinary psychiatric hospital and Mr Borisov be retained in the Leningrad special psychiatric hospital.[127]

By 1974, many of the political inmates of Soviet psychiatric hospitals about whom most is known outside the USSR had either been released (for example, Pyotr Grigorenko, Victor Fainberg, Vladimir Borisov, Vladimir Gershuni) or transferred from special to ordinary psychiatric hospitals (for example Mikhail Kukobaka, Pyotr Starchik, Anatoly Ponomaryov). This must be acknowledged to be a positive and welcome step, and the hope was encouraged that, despite the continued incarceration of Leonid Plyushch and a number of other known political inmates, the practice of confining persons in psychiatric hospitals because of their political or religious views had been modified.

However, recent reports emanating from the USSR indicates that this practice is still in application. Issues 32 and 34 of the *samizdat A Chronicle of Current Events* recorded a number of recent cases of persons being confined to psychiat-

123. "On the Special Psycniatric Hospitals ('Fools' Houses')", in P.G. Grigorenko, *Myslyi Sumasshedshego*, (Herzen Foundation: Amsterdam, 1973), page 241.
124. *A Chronicle of Current Events*, number 18, page 109.
125. Ibid, number 25, page 205.
126. Ibid, number 27, page 315.
127. Ibid, Number 27, note 63.

ric hospitals in connection with charges relating to their having expressed officially disapproved of views. *The New York Times* reported in 1974 the case of Svetlana Shramko, a resident of Ryazan (south of Moscow) who had been committed to a psychiatric hospital in June 1974 in connection with her public protests against pollution caused by a local factory.[128] Number 35 of *A Chronicle of Current Events* (March 1975) reported the case of Boris Vinokurov, a Soviet radio and television official confined to a psychiatric hospital five days after urging at a Communist Party meeting the creation of a two-party system in the USSR.[129] In March 1975, Reuter reported from Moscow that Vladimir Osipov, former editor of the Slavophile *samizdat* journals *Veche* and *Zemlya,* had been sent to the Serbksy Institute for forensic psychiatric diagnosis in connection with official charges of "anti-Soviet agitation and propaganda".[130]

128. See *The New York Times,* 30 September 1974.
129. Cited in *The Sunday Telegraph* (London), 4 May 1975.
130. Reuter news agency dispatch, 30 March 1975.

# Recommendations

In the light of the disturbing treatment and conditions of prisoners of conscience in the USSR detailed in the preceding chapters, Amnesty International is putting forward the following recommendations to the Soviet government and to Soviet lawyers and penologists. These recommendations fall into two categories: those regarding Soviet corrective labour institutions and those regarding compulsory detention on psychiatric grounds.

## With Regard to Corrective Labour Institutions:

As this report has shown, the Soviet corrective labour system not only violates international standards for the treatment of prisoners, but fails to achieve the standards established in parts of domestic corrective labour legislation and theory. In this it is not unique, insofar as few prison systems operate without inhumanity. This does not absolve Soviet policy-makers of the responsibility to take strong actions towards improving the treatment of prisoners.

**1. Amnesty International RECOMMENDS that the Soviet government open the corrective labour system to careful and public scrutiny with an aim to instituting a program of penal reform.**

In a number of countries and at different times, penal reform has been a subject of open and widespread debate. Such debates normally focus on harsh prison conditions and on the practical inefficacy of some penal methods. Public concern usually springs both from the principle that society as a whole is responsible to those of its members who, as prisoners, are particularly vulnerable and from a pragmatic concern that imprisonment, being expensive, should give some return to society in terms of prevention of crime.

Soviet authorities have often noted the value of public discussion on important matters of policy. In the mid-1960s, Soviet publications provided space for a discussion of the form which the then pending corrective labour legislation should take. Unfortunately, this public discussion has since been brought to a close and the penal system is now rarely mentioned in the Soviet mass media. Some debate on the nature of the corrective labour system has continued among Soviet jurists and criminologists, but it has not resulted in improvement of conditions. Until now, the subject has been treated as virtually a state secret, as is witnessed by the almost total absence in the Soviet media and professional publications of factual reports of penal conditions and the almost unbroken official refusal to acknowledge the existence of serious abuses. This official secrecy not only fails to distract public and international attention from real abuses, but also encourages the widespread belief that the contemporary Soviet prison system retains all the worst features of its past. As long as this secrecy remains, the prison system will continue to generate suspicion and mistrust, certainly abroad and to some extent within the Soviet Union itself.

A systematic and open review of the Soviet corrective labour system is urgently required because of the punitive, vindictive attitude which dominates the official interpretation and application of the corrective labour law. This attitude appears to extend into the USSR Council of Ministers, which is responsible for determining the reprehensibly low food rations for prisoners. Disrespect for the interests of prisoners is particularly strong in the Ministry of Internal Affairs (MVD) which administers the corrective labour system, and appears to prevail at all its levels down to the staffs of corrective labour institutions, with a negative effect on numerous aspects of the treatment of prisoners.

Soviet policy-makers' attention should be drawn to the fact that in current corrective labour practice reliance is consistently placed not on the correction or re-education of prisoners but on punishing them both as a form of retribution and as a means of deterring them and others from committing "socially dangerous" actions. It is not accidental but part of official policy that the present system of material provision for prisoners entails their being subjected to daily hunger and medical neglect. This manifestation of official intention to punish prisoners so determines the situation of the latter that it dislodges correction and re-education as the goals of the corrective labour system.

The programs established to correct and re-educate prisoners serve less to reform prisoners than to add to their punishment. For example, the conditions of compulsory labour are such that they discourage rather than enhance the official aim of rehabilitating prisoners. This applies alike to prisoners of conscience and to those imprisoned for ordinary criminal offences. Prisoners of conscience are likewise victims rather than beneficiaries of political re-education practices in their present form. Prisoners of conscience generally emerge from corrective labour institutions effectively disqualified from taking employment compatible with any technical or professional skills which they might possess.

In the recommended public reappraisal of the Soviet corrective labour system, close attention should be paid to this phenomenon and to its impact on the system's achievement of its officially prescribed goals and of the humanitarian standards demanded of it in parts of Soviet law. As long as the present attitude toward prisoners is maintained in decisive official organs, the abuses described in this report will persist.

**2. Amnesty International RECOMMENDS the strengthening of the agencies responsible for supervision of the observance of legality within the corrective labour system.**

At present the Ministry of Internal Affairs and its subordinate institutions are allowed too much discretion in the administration and operation of corrective labour institutions. This situation is made particularly dangerous by the punitive attitude toward prisoners which prevails at all levels of the Ministry of Internal Affairs. It is in large measure due to these two factors that prisoners usually are required to work under conditions in which little regard has been paid to the safety and health standards established by law. There is considerable evidence that in recent years the treatment of prisoners, especially prisoners of conscience, has worsened significantly. This deterioration has come about largely via administrative regulations issued by the MVD. Many of these changes are enabled by vagueness and omission of detail in the corrective labour legislation. Some appear to be in direct violation of the provisions of that legislation. This is true, for example, of the relatively recent rule which effectively makes it compulsory for prisoners to attend political re-education classes and which places new restrictions on prisoners' right to lodge formal complaints.

Soviet law recognizes the need for regular and independent supervision of the operations of corrective labour institutions and provides the procuracy and the public supervisory commissions with the legal authority to fulfil these functions. Unfortunately, until now these agencies have been either unable or unwilling to check the many systematic and disturbing abuses. They should be granted whatever increased authority is necessary to enable them to fulfil the tasks set for them by law with regard to the corrective labour system.

**3.** This report has discussed the Soviet corrective labour system in terms of domestic Soviet legislation. In view of our findings, we believe that in approaching reform of the corrective labour system, Soviet policy-makers should consider that some abuses emanate from deficiencies in the law itself. The currently operative corrective labour legislation does not proscribe the "infliction of suffering" on prisoners. While it proclaims that infliction of suffering and degradation are not the goal of the corrective labour system, it enables these to occupy the central place in the treatment of prisoners, for example by legitimizing the subjection of prisoners to permanent hunger and by failing to require adequate medical treatment for the physical ailments which regularly afflict prisoners as a consequence of poor feeding provisions and overwork.

Internationally endorsed criteria useful for any reform of Soviet penal law exist in the form of the United Nations' Standard Minimum Rules for the Treatment of Prisoners,[1] which Soviet authorities have publicly accepted as representing realistic standards for conditions in penal institutions. In this report we have detailed systematic violations of a number of the Standard Minimum Rules, including Rules 6, 17(1), 20(1), 25, 26, 27, 32, 36, 37, 45(2), 48, 57, 71(1), 74(1). (The texts of these rules are reproduced in an appendix to this report.)

**Amnesty International RECOMMENDS that the Soviet authorities take immediate steps to implement all of the UN Standard Minimum Rules for the Treatment of Prisoners, amending the Soviet law where it conflicts with the Standard Minimum Rules and taking strict regard for the spirit in which they were written, as well as for their specific provisions.**

1. UN Document A/CONF/6/1, Annex A.

## With Regard to Compulsory Detention on Psychiatric Grounds:

The area of mental health and illness is the most difficult within which to make recommendations. It is simple to illustrate and condemn examples of abuses of existing procedures, but more complex to propose a formula which would prevent such abuses, or to find proposals which would effectively safeguard the interest of the individual. One principle may be stated: no one should, because of allegations of mental illness, be deprived of legal, medical or procedural safeguards which would be available to him if he were well. Anyone accused of an offence or suspected of mental illness must be legally able to influence all decisions affecting him. This capacity must be guaranteed him not only during the investigation period and at the time of the court hearing of his case, but throughout his confinement to a psychiatric institution. Failure to guarantee the accused such capacity represents unnecessary and undesirable degradation of persons judged by others to be mentally ill, and invites wrongful confinement and improper medical treatment of individuals.

1. **Amnesty International RECOMMENDS that Soviet legislation be so revised as to include the following:**

a. The following rights, guaranteed for accused persons in Article 46 of the RSFSR Code of Criminal Procedure, should also be preserved for accused persons whose mental health is called into question:

> The accused shall have the right to know what he is accused of and to give explanations concerning the accusation presented to him; to present evidence; to submit petitions; to become acquainted with all the materials of the case upon completion of the preliminary investigation or inquiry; to have defence counsel from the moment provided for by Article 47 of the present code; to participate in the judicial examination in the court of first instance; to submit challenges; and to appeal from the actions and decisions of the person conducting the inquiry, the investigator, procurator, and court.[2]

b. The accused person whose mental health is called into question should be informed of the official (legal or medical) decisions affecting his case at every step of the process. All rights of accused persons established by Articles 184 and 185 of the RSFSR Code of Criminal Procedure (relating to the procedure of conducting expert examinations) should be extended to accused persons subjected to forensic psychiatric examination. Specifically, Article 184 should be amended to exclude its paragraph 4:

> The decree to assign a forensic psychiatric expert examination and the opinion of the experts shall not be announced to the accused if his mental state makes this impossible.

c. Such an accused person should be guaranteed regular communication with a lawyer of his own or his family's choice and with his family and immediate

2. Here as in the text of this Report, the RSFSR Criminal Code and the RSFSR Code of Criminal Procedure are quoted as translated into the English language in Harold J. Berman and James W. Spindler (translators), *Soviet Criminal Law and Procedure: The RSFSR Codes* (Harvard University Press, Cambridge, Massachusetts, 1972).

friends. In the present RSFSR Code of Criminal Procedure (Article 405), defence counsel "is permitted to participate in a case from the moment the fact of the mental illness of the person who has committed the socially dangerous act is established" — that is, from the moment a forensic psychiatric commission has declared its opinion to this effect. This legal norm leaves the accused person without defence counsel at one of the most decisive moments of his case (the psychiatric examination), and should be altered to allow participation of defence counsel from the moment at which investigation officials decide to submit the accused person to psychiatric examination. With regard to communication between the accused person and his defence counsel, there should be strict adherence to Article 12, paragraph 2 of the Statute on Remand in Custody (USSR Supreme Soviet, 11 July 1969):

> From the moment when the defence counsel is allowed to take part in the case, this being confirmed by a written communication of the person or body in charge of the case, the committed persons shall have the right to private visits by their defence counsel without any restriction on the number of visits and their duration.

d. An accused person whose mental health has been called into question (or his family) should be able to influence the composition of any forensic psychiatric commission examining him. This requires application to such cases of Article 185, point (2) of the RSFSR Code of Criminal Procedure, which guarantees to accused persons the right "to request the assignment of an expert from among persons indicated by them". A mechanism should be established to enable such an accused person to obtain the withdrawal from the examining commission of psychiatrists whom he (or his family) regards as incompetent or prejudiced against him.

e. The accused person should be present during the conduct of the expert psychiatric diagnosis, and he should retain the right to question and challenge the examining psychiatrists, as provided for most types of expert examinations by Article 185 of the RSFSR Code of Criminal Procedure.

f. Court hearings on the mental state of defendants under criminal law should be open to the public in accordance with the general provision of Soviet law. The defendant should be allowed to appear in the court hearing on his case, unless it can be shown that he would disrupt the court proceedings through violence. If, as should happen only in exceptional cases, the defendant does not appear in court, his viewpoint should be put in court in the form of written statements composed by himself for that purpose. In any event, he should invariably be represented in court not only by a lawyer chosen by himself or his family (and with whom he has had regular contact), but also by representatives of his family or by an acquaintance of his own choosing.

g. In cases where the accused (or his family) does not accept the findings of the forensic psychiatric commission, he should be able to draw to the attention of the court the findings of a second, independent psychiatric examination.

h. The defendant and his lawyer should have access to any judicial file concerning his case and in the possession of the prosecution or court.

i. The defendant and representatives of his family should be able to appeal against a court ruling and be able to attend the appellate court hearing. He (they) should at this stage again be able to bring into evidence the findings of a psychiatric commission of his (their) choice.

j. Stringent criteria should be developed to assist courts in their decisions as to the type of measures to be taken with regard to persons judged to be mentally ill. Courts should use more frequently the option (provided in Article 60 of the RSFSR Criminal Code) of transferring such persons to the care of their relatives or guardians. A person judged to be mentally ill should be ordered to be confined to a special (maximum security) psychiatric institution only if it can be clearly shown that, on account of his mental condition, his continued presence in society represents an immediate and violent threat to himself or others.

k. At present there is, to Amnesty International's knowledge, no public legal act which makes clear which of his rights a Soviet citizen retains if he is confined to a psychiatric hospital for compulsory treatment. This should be rectified by introducing to legal codes explicit statements that inmates of psychiatric institutions possess certain rights, among the latter being:

I.   The right of the inmate and his family to appeal at any time or at regular intervals to an authority independent of the hospital staff and administration and empowered to stop further compulsory treatment and compulsory hospitalization.

II.   The right of the inmate to have regular contact with his family and with a lawyer.

III.   The right of the inmate to communicate (undisturbed and uncensored by hospital authorities) to the procuracy any complaints or grievances regarding his treatment in the hospital or the process by which he came to be in the hospital, a right accorded to all Soviet citizens by the decree "On the Procedure for Review of Citizens' Proposals, Application and Complaints" (Presidium of the USSR Supreme Soviet, 12 April 1968), but in practice denied to inmates of psychiatric hospitals.

l. The administrative provision (in the 1967 "Instruction on the System of Application of Compulsory Treatment and Other Measures of Medical Character in Relation to Mentally Ill Persons Who Have Committed Socially Dangerous Acts") for regular six-monthly re-examinations of psychiatric patients is laudable, but does not go far enough to provide any real guarantee that healthy or recovered inmates will be released from psychiatric institutions. It should be required in law that such commissions include representatives of the procuracy, empowered to protest against the recommendations made by the psychiatric commission. The inmate should be represented at the deliberation of such commissions by a lawyer and by members of his family or by an acquaintance of his own choosing.

**2. The instructions governing conditions in and operating methods of psychiatric institutions should be reassessed. Amnesty International RECOMMENDS that such Instructions be revised to preclude the numerous practical abuses described in the present Report and that these Instructions be published and made easily accessible to the general public and to concerned parties.**

**3. Amnesty International RECOMMENDS that the rights of inmates of psychiat-**

ric hospitals be extended to allow them and their families decisive influence in their medical treatment. Psychiatrists should be required to consult patients or their families before applying any type of medical treatment. The patients and their families should have the right and the practical possibility to consult psychiatrists and doctors working outside the given psychiatric institution, seeking their advice both as to the patient's condition and as to the efficacy of whatever treatments the patient has received. Patients or their families should have the right to turn down any specific form of medical treatment according to the principle established for general medical practice in Article 35 of the Fundamentals of Public Health Legislation of the USSR and Union Republics:

> Surgical operations shall be performed and complex methods of diagnosis applied with the consent of the patients and in the case of the sick below 16 years of age and the mentally deranged with the consent of their parents, guardians or trustees.

If there must be exceptions to this rule, these should be carefully defined in the operative instructions for psychiatric institutions, which should be made public. Patients and their relatives should be able to initiate criminal or civil court proceedings against any hospital staff member whom they believe to have abused their authority: attendants who have maltreated patients, doctors who, for non-therapeutic reasons, have made wrong diagnoses or prescribed wrong treatment, administrators who have obstructed patients' or relatives' efforts to seek change in the existing situation. Such proceedings should be made public.

# Appendix

*Excerpts from the United Nations' Standard Minimum Rules for the Treatment of Prisoners.*

Amnesty International has found in Soviet corrective labour practice regular violation of a number of provisions of the United Nations' Standard Minimum Rules for the Treatment of Prisoners, among them the following:

6. (1) The following rules shall be applied impartially. There shall be no discrimination on grounds of race, colour, sex, language, religion, political or other opinion, national or social origin, property, birth or other status.
(2) On the other hand, it is necessary to respect the religious beliefs and moral precepts of the group to which a prisoner belongs.

17. (1) Every prisoner who is not allowed to wear his own clothing shall be provided with an outfit of clothing suitable for the climate and adequate to keep him in good health. Such clothing shall in no manner be degrading or humiliating.

20. (1) Every prisoner shall be provided by the administration at the usual hours with food of nutritional value adequate for health and strength, of wholesome quality and well prepared and served.

25. (1) The medical officer shall have the care of the physical and mental health of the prisoners and should daily see all sick prisoners, all who complain of illness, and any prisoner to whom his attention is specially directed.
(2) The medical officer shall report to the director whenever he considers that a prisoner's physical or mental health has been or will be injuriously affected by continued imprisonment or by any condition of imprisonment.

26. (1)  The medical officer shall regularly inspect and advise the director upon:
   (a)  The quantity, quality, preparation and service of food;
   (b)  The hygiene and cleanliness of the institution and the prisoners;
   (c)  The sanitation, heating, lighting and ventilation of the institution;
   (d)  The suitability and cleanliness of the prisoners' clothing and bedding;
   (e)  The observance of the rules concerning physical education and sports, in cases where there is no technical personnel in charge of these activities.

(2)  The director shall take into consideration the reports and advice that the medical officer submits according to rules 25(2) and 26 and, in case he concurs with the recommendations made, shall take immediate steps to give effect to those recommendations; if they are not within his competence or if he does not concur with them, he shall immediately submit his own report and the advice of the medical officer to higher authority.

27.  Discipline and order shall be maintained with firmness, but with no more restriction than is necessary for safe custody and well-ordered community life.

32. (1)  Punishment by close confinement or reduction of diet shall never be inflicted unless the medical officer has examined the prisoner and certified in writing that he is fit to sustain it.

(2)  The same shall apply to any other punishment that may be prejudicial to the physical or mental health of a prisoner. In no case may such punishment be contrary to or depart from the principle stated in rule 31.

(3)  The medical officer shall visit daily prisoners undergoing such punishments and shall advise the director if he considers the termination or alteration of the punishment necessary on grounds of physical or mental health.

36. (1)  Every prisoner shall have the opportunity each weekday of making requests or complaints to the director of the institution or the officer authorized to represent him.

(2)  It shall be possible to make requests or complaints to the inspector of prisons during his inspection. The prisoner shall have the opportunity to talk to the inspector or to any other inspecting officer without the director or other members of the staff being present.

(3)  Every prisoner shall be allowed to make a request or complaint, without censorship as to substance but in proper form, to the central prison administration, the judicial authority or other proper authorities through approved channels.

(4)   Unless it is evidently frivolous or groundless, every request or complaint shall be promptly dealt with and replied to without undue delay.

37. Prisoners shall be allowed under necessary supervision to communicate with their family and reputable friends at regular intervals, both by correspondence and by receiving visits.

45. (2)   The transport of prisoners in conveyances with inadequate ventilation or light, or in any way which would subject them to unnecessary physical hardship, shall be prohibited.

48. All members of the personnel shall at all times so conduct themselves and perform their duties as to influence the prisoners for good by their examples and to command their respect.

57. Imprisonment and other measures which result in cutting off an offender from the outside world are afflictive by the very fact of taking from the person the right of self-determination by depriving him of his liberty. Therefore the prison system shall not, except as incidental to justifiable segregation or the maintenance of discipline, aggravate the suffering inherent in such a situation.

71. (1)   Prison labour must not be of an afflictive nature.

74. (1)   The precautions laid down to protect the safety and health of free workmen shall be equally observed in institutions.

## АССОЦИАЦИЯ СОВЕТСКИХ ЮРИСТОВ
## ASSOCIATION DES JURISTES SOVIETIQUES

МОСКВА, К-9
ПРОСПЕКТ КАЛИНИНА, 14

14, AVENUE KALININE,
MOSCOU K-9
U. R.S.S.

" 2 7 " ____VIII_____ 197 5 г.

№ _____

Mr. Martin Ennals
Secretary General of
Amnesty international

53, Theobald's Road
London WCIX 8SP

Dear Sir,

In connection with your letter dated April, 15 th and
so-called "Report of Conditions of Detention of Prisoniers of
Conscience" We would like to acknowlege you that ar we not eager
to discass about what you call a book and that is vulgar falsi-
fication and defamation on Soviet reality and socialist legeti-
macy.

Sincerely,    *I. Смирнов*.

L. Smirnov

President of the Soviet
Lawyer's Association

# INDEX

*Numbers in brackets after names refer to the page on which a photograph of the person may be found*

150

154